For my husband, Jed,
who listened when the angels
brought us together.
I love you, and so do they.

Contents

Acknowledgments

ngels abound when it comes to putting together a book such as *Divine Nudges*. In addition to my loving mother, Dorothy Lanigan; my sister, Nancy Porter; my brothers, Ed and Robert Lanigan; my son, Ryan Pieszchala; my daughter-in-law, Christy Pieszchala, my grandaughter, Caylin Pieszchala; my nephews, Ben Porter and Sam Porter; my nieces Karen, Elizabeth, Meghan, Maureen and Cathleen Lanigan and Elaine Perez; my sisters-in-law Mary and Debbie Lanigan; my sister-in-law Susie Garrison; and my brother-in-law, David Porter, I send bouquets of appreciation and blessings from my soul to: Vicki Bushman; Roger Burlage; Alex Bunshaft; Julie Culver, my literary agent; Sande and Mark Donahue; Ray Ebberman; Judy Fry; Cherry Hickson; Jenni and Brad Hummel; Carol and Bob Kane; Jim and Clare Keating; Audra Kelly; Sabina Khan; John Kissonas; Wendy and Tommy Korman; my manager, Vicki McCarty; Joanna Plafsky; Sharon Reese; Tom and Kelly Schmidt; Dea Shandera; my film agent, Dean Schram;

Stacy Stoker; and my literary agent, Nancy Yost.

I would also like to sincerely thank all the HCI angels who have allowed me to continue on this very divine path: president and resident angel, Peter Vegso; my very special editor, Amy Hughes; soul-sisters Kim Weiss and Kelly Maragni; and sales' battling angels Terry Burke and Tom Sand.

My heartfelt gratitude may not be enough thanks for all you have done for me. I am honored to have all of you in my past, present and future. God bless you all.

Introduction

y inspiration for this book came from you.

In the years since the publication of my first book on the subject of angels and life on the Other Side, *Angel Watch: Goosebumps, Signs, Dreams and Divine Nudges,* I have been struck by the remarkable reaction from its readers. On book tours for subsequent novels, there have always been a substantial number of readers who come to me and want to talk about their experiences with their own personal angels. Their inspiration has been the impetus for this second collection of stories about people's interactions with angels.

It is my belief and experience that angels are all around us performing miracles both big and small, most of which we never acknowledge. We call these fortunate incidences "good luck" or "coincidences," or sometimes we label them as "mishaps." Most of us rarely give credit to the divine in our lives at all.

We human beings take credit for just about anything and

everything that goes our way. If things go badly, we invariably blame someone else. We have a tendency not to take responsibility for the "bad" things that happen in our lives. The fact that we call challenges and frustrations "bad" is a prime example of our lack of vision into our own human experience.

How many times have you gotten out of bed and no matter what you did that morning, everything worked against you to make you late for work? The water pressure in the shower, which had always been strong, was suddenly very low, and you spent an extra five minutes in the shower rinsing the shampoo from your hair. The electric shaver went on the fritz. You blew the breaker box. You spilled juice on your skirt, and that forced you to change your entire outfit. You broke your heel, the back door would not lock properly, the security system wouldn't work, and finally, for some reason, you couldn't get the key into the ignition. Some of these annoying trials can be explained, but why wouldn't a car key work in the ignition?

The story above is a short synopsis of a workday morning that my sister, Nancy Porter, experienced about a decade ago. I tell this story in my first book.

Nancy was perplexed as to why all this was happening to her. She was a grown woman who had been driving a car for twenty years. How tough was it to put a key in an ignition and start the car? She told me that it was as if an invisible hand had kept her from inserting the key into the ignition. Nancy went into her house, and a few hours later turned on the television news. She was stunned to see that a deadly ice storm had moved into the Chicago area, and there were several very severe accidents on I-94 West, heading into the city. It was precisely the route Nancy would have taken. She immediately said a prayer of thanksgiving. Nancy has always credited this incident to her "angels" saving her from what could have been a very serious accident.

We have all experienced these small and not-so-small miracles. Some of us have been blessed with lifesaving, death-defying angelic interventions. Some of us have actually seen winged beings or Beings of Light that have not only changed our lives, but altered our way of thinking forever.

For a long time, people have feared ridicule and have not spoken about these kinds of eerie or strange occurrences in their lives. No one wants to be labeled a "kook" by his or her friends or family. For the most part, we have kept our mouths shut and just gone on with our lives, pretending that "nothing happened," or we tell ourselves that it was our imagination. We blame our imagination for the supernatural, somehow believing that if we ignore the "unseen" world, it will go away.

What a sad commentary on modern man.

Ancient humans had no difficulty at all acknowledging the divine in their lives. Our tribal ancestors spoke often about the interaction between the real world and the life beyond "the Veil." The energy field that separates our "see it, feel it, taste it" reality from the spiritual realm in which our departed friends and relatives, as well as the angels, cherubim and seraphim exist, is simply an energy field or "veil" of a higher vibration.

I am not a physicist or an expert on quantum physics, and I leave all those explanations to the scientists. What I am is a chronicler of occurrences, incidents and happenings that are collected in this book as evidence of another world of existence that parallels our own. My purpose in writing this second book is to push the edges of the envelope that I opened in *Angel Watch*. I believe, and have been told by angels, that this is part of my divine path. It's not my entire destiny, but it's a huge chunk of it.

In *Angel Watch* I described my father's near-death experience and his later interaction with the spiritual world as he lay dying in the hospital with my mother and me at his side, three days before his actual death.

In 1987, when my father "died" for twenty minutes in a hospital with a team of doctors banging on his chest, breaking his sternum and all his ribs trying to revive him, he came back from that experience and told me that he had met a "Being of Light" from "the Other Side." My father was a staunch Catholic and raised us all as Catholics. Catholics refer to heaven as heaven. It is not paradise, which is a Protestant word, and it certainly is not referred to as "the Other Side."

When I asked him if he saw an angel, he adamantly replied. "No, Cathy, it was a Being of Light."

"Did you see Jesus?" I asked.

"No. It was a Being of Light."

All of this was strange to me, though I had begun to hear such terms by 1987, when Daddy suffered his heart attack. Just the fact that this very, very Catholic man came back from the dead and told me that he had been to the Other Side and that he had seen this Being, was, for me, the truth.

Daddy went on to say that from that time on, I was to change my writing. I was to write stories, books, novels, films, anything in which I told about the interplay of humans and angels, however minute those roles in the finished product might be. The essence of the message must always be embedded in the words I write.

I also thought it was interesting that from this time on, my father referred to people as "human beings." My father had been a World War II hero and a captain in the army. He was an attorney and had graduated from Notre Dame Law School. He was Phi Beta Kappa and literally the most intelligent man I'd ever met. He had an incredible brain and never lost his brainpower even as he lay dying.

From 1987 to 1992, when he died on Valentine's Day, he spoke about people as "human beings" to distinguish them in his mind from the other kinds of beings, those spiritual beings he had seen from the Other Side.

On this information alone, as far as I was concerned, I now had validation for my childhood "visits" from angels and departed relatives, even though at the time my mother and father had attributed them to my "overactive imagination."

Today, many of us know this was not and is not imagination.

These "beings" were and are real.

One of my purposes in *Divine Nudges* is to relate my near-death experiences. I was in surgery, and this information goes far beyond anything that I have previously described in a book or in my lectures.

I believe that my father's near-death experience was the spiritual world's way of preparing me for what was about to happen to me and for the messages and information I was going to be given.

I think it is interesting that in the past few years our media has suddenly begun to embrace, with a passion, our spiritual lives. Just last night as I was watching a network television program, *NYPD Blue*, the story line had Jimmy Smits's character (who had died in an earlier episode) returning to interact with his friends. The dialogue between Jimmy Smits and Dennis Franz was nearly letter perfect to what I have been told during such situations in my own life. They reflected the same sentiments and facts as the hundreds of e-mails I have received from readers over the past several years that relate the messages they have received from angels.

The themes are almost always the same.

We are not alone.

God loves us all, no matter what.

Our departed family members and friends are standing right beside us willing to guide us, talk to us, help us in any way that they can.

The Other Side is a place of peace, love and yes, work. Our family members work every day just as we do, except their work often seems to be concerned with convincing us that they exist!

As I discussed in my last book, angels and "light beings" try to reach us through our dreams and meditations. They give us signs and validations via goose bumps, flickering lights and unusual sounds, such as taps on a windowpane. As we have evolved in our humanness to become more aware of our own uniqueness and divinity, the angels and spiritual beings have been making their presence blatantly known.

For those of you who are creative, whether your works have seen the inside of an art gallery, a stage, a theater or have been printed in a book or not, many of you are more aware than ever that our "inspiration" is not a matter of ego, but a matter of divine intervention. So many authors, screenwriters and filmmakers that I meet every day are sharing the same observations. They know that the words and visions we receive are coming *through* us.

We are all the vessels for God's work. Our work must "mean" something not only for today but also for future generations. We truly want to leave the world a better place.

To do that, we must allow thoughts of the divine to flow through us. After that, we must acknowledge the "source" of our ideas. No matter what the religion or faith, there is a "spiritual wiring" mechanism in the essence of our human makeup that predisposes us to believe there is a God or Higher Intelligence that rules the universe.

This goes not just for artists, but also for every man, woman and child on earth. We are all creative people. Creativity is a large component of our souls. Too many times I have heard people at my lectures say, "But I'm not creative at all." How far from the truth this is!

Everyone is creative and talented at something. Some of us can grow flowers in a rock garden. Some of us have a talent for being the best kind of friend a person could have. Some are great parents. Some are great parents to pets. None of us is everything to everyone. We are all individuals, but we are all creative. It is time for us all to acknowledge our innate creativity.

In the past few years, there have been many articles in major newsmagazines (*Time, Newsweek*) in which the subject of mind-body-soul connectedness has been explored. More than half the American population in the past year sought holistic or alternative medicine remedies for everything from headache to cancer. The fact that so many of our citizens are seeking acupuncture, meditation, yoga, nutritional guidance, acupressure and alternative therapies reveals that as a people we realize there is more to human existence than just our physical bodies. One cannot go through this life and deny the divinity of our makeup any longer. Ancient man knew this. How is it that we forgot?

The answer is simple: too much in our present life gets in our way.

Americans especially, but all citizens of modern, industrialized, high-tech, Internet-connected countries from Brazil to France, Russia, China and India can relate. When was the last time you went outside on a summer night and watched the stars or fireflies . . . for any length of time?

When was the last time you simply sat and stared at the blazing fire in your fireplace? How many Americans have replaced their wood-burning fireplaces with gas logs thinking they have eliminated a time-consuming "mess" from their lives? The truth is that even the last generation after World War II didn't put fireplaces in their homes to keep them warm. They had a furnace to do that. The fireplace was there to add warmth, both physical and mental. It was there to look at. To stare into. To contemplate the day. To dream of the future.

Few of us today spend any time dreaming of our futures. We don't make plans for our lives. We're too busy "just getting through the day." We are "putting out fires," not contemplating them.

In the flames of a simple holiday fireplace we make the traditions that will become for many of us the framework of our future. Perhaps we have always wanted to write a book or stage play, but we had to bathe, dress and pick the kids up from school with that time. Have you thought about the legacy you would leave your children if you took those hours away from watching the football game or *Oprah* and used the time to write down or put structure to that idea that might become the foundation of a new business that your children might inherit? What if your child wanted to become an artist? Thirty years ago such an announcement would have sent parents scurrying for yet another savings account for their child because only the most gifted artists could earn a living.

Today, the film world looms on the edge of the extinction of the live actor. In less than five years, graphic artists and cartoonists and special effects artists will have perfected the process in which animation will depict a human on film that looks and acts like a human. The first glimpse of this superior advance in film technology is *Polar Express,* the 2004 Christmas film.

A child today who wants to draw and believes in his heart that he was put on earth to draw, no longer has to take a "day job" to feed himself. The possibilities for the next generation in computer artistry will be limitless.

There are some who say that the angels have abandoned us.

I believe that due to the acceleration in our technology, including, but not limited to, our voyages to other planets, that angels are busier than ever delving into our lives and making certain we are all on our divine path. We just don't take the time to see them.

Make the time.

This book is dedicated to bringing out true stories, as inconceivable as they may appear, to the light of our real world. I have expanded my sources for stories to friends, like Vicki Bushman, who finally has given me the green light to tell the story about the day the "dark forces" came to take her baby son, Andrew, away from her and how she conquered "the angels of death" through her own will and belief in God.

In some stories you will find aspects that are a bit more unsettling than the stories you read in my first book on this subject, *Angel Watch*. However, I believe that we have all grown in our spirituality in the past few years. Certainly, in the United States, our lives have been greatly realigned and redefined since September 11, 2001. Many of us appreciate every breath we take just a little bit more. That smile on our child's face glows just a smidgeon brighter. The chance that we have to hug our elderly aunt or cousin who never gave us the time of day has become a very precious gesture, and we know that we might not have the opportunity next week to hug her. She or *you* may have perished by then.

You should live every day as if it were your last. Though that is clichéd, it is true. This doesn't mean you should throw caution to the wind and go on a binge or party every day with no responsibilities. It does mean that you may not have the chance tomorrow to tell the ones you love all that they mean to you. If you get a chance to be nice to someone, do it. Just to recognize a person by saying "hello" is a kindness. A busboy, the janitor at your work, people who are almost always invisible, by just acknowledging them, letting them know how much you appreciate what they do, you can perform a kindness that is more meaningful than you might realize. If you have the chance to say, "I love you," to a friend or relative or be courteous to a stranger, do it. Live every second of your life in love.

If your perspective of your life has not altered in this fashion, then it is my prayer that this book will help do that for you.

If it has been difficult for you to remember the friend you pushed away many years ago, or if you just can't forgive Uncle Sal for his verbal abuse of you when you were twelve years old, perhaps now you can see that your bitterness is your creation, and you are only hurting yourself.

Your angels want you to live fully and completely in love and joy. You can't get to that kind of a wondrous place with pain and anger still in your heart.

Open your eyes to the stories in this book. Open your heart to God's love around you. Be the kind of person you want other people to be to you.

The next time when you hear that "voice" in your head and feel the nudge to say and do the right thing, the blessings will be yours, and the effects will be divine.

Divine Nudges

n this book, *divine nudges* are not a gentle reminder that you need to try a little harder to be a bit kinder to your friend or family member. To be honest, if only we all did precisely that much every day of our lives *all day long,* we just might stop war and domestic violence and empty our prisons. Divine nudges in our stories are "divine get-a-clue" situations that drastically alter our lives, our career paths and our relationships *for the good.*

These moments may be what many would consider traumatic: sudden loss of employment, divorce or romantic breakup, sudden death of a partner, death of a best friend, unexpected job relocation, tragic loss of a dwelling due to fire, flood, earthquake, hurricane or tsunami, or a very serious health issue.

Just to give one example of how divine nudges can help people get to a better place in their lives, look at the area of domestic violence.

For over two decades I have worked with, spoken out for and supported in my own way the victims of domestic violence. For these women and their abused children, escaping their violent husbands or boyfriends is incredibly traumatic. As horrific as their lives are inside the walls of abuse, it *is* their comfort zone. Most women stay in these marriages and relationships for financial security or because their religion teaches they cannot divorce. For some, it is family pressure that makes them stay. They are told that the embarrassment of a divorce is greater than the physical violence or verbal threats to the abused victim. In far too many instances, the woman fears that her husband will murder her or the children if she leaves. Too many times, these threats are real.

When an abused woman finally finds the courage to escape her abuser, the alteration in her life requires substantial angelic intervention. It may happen on the day when her husband has threatened physical violence and finally hits her.

She is bruised and bleeding, but she leaves him shortly thereafter. For years she has tolerated verbal abuse. She has been "put down" in public. Most abusers cut their victim's ability to communicate with their family or friends. Abusers are possessive and obsessive. They demand to be made the center of the universe. It is "their way or the highway." To maintain control, abusers must "up the ante" over a period of years until the time comes when they reach their boiling point and physical violence becomes their next step.

Many times circumstances that to the victims of abuse seem completely out of their control occur that cause the abuser to explode. This explosion can be quite violent. However, this eruption is the very moment of the divine nudge. The victim must finally make a decision, on her own, to leave. She can't go back anymore. She can't take it anymore, and her only option is to leave.

Once she is out on her own, she begins to think of her life with all new rules, parameters and options. She has begun to live *her* life for herself by her rules.

The victim then realizes that she has been "nudged" from a negative plane of existence to a much higher plane of love and abundance. She must realize she can "live without him" and his money. Most importantly, *she must believe in herself* enough to face the world alone. This woman's life and those of her children, if she has any, have been greatly "nudged" into a divine sphere.

A divine nudge happens fairly quickly. The situation portrayed in the Broadway play *The Fantasticks* is a divine nudge. A boy and girl live next door to each other, and though they love each other, their love is untested.

A carnival comes to town, and in the space of forty-eight hours, the heroine is romanced by a "carny" who promises to show her exotic, foreign-sounding places. The hero is jumped and beaten by thugs, and during his incarceration he thinks only of the heroine. He realizes his love for her is very strong. It is enough to give him the courage to escape, no matter what the consequences. Once reunited, they both realize they nearly lost each other. Infused with the realization of the power of this love for each other, they vow never to take the other for granted again. Within the space of two short days, the perspective of their lives is drastically altered.

A divine nudge occurs when a total stranger enters your life for only a brief moment or a single day and shows you the tools of your talent or a destiny that perhaps you didn't even know you had or that has been lying dormant for years.

Divine nudges are meant to keep your universe in divine order.

The Angelic Traffic Ticket

*T*he mystical meetings humans endlessly dream about the most are those of finding true soul mates. This desire is the fuel of movies, books, songs and music videos. There is some deep well in the human psyche that tells even the most skeptical of cynics that somewhere—out there—is a single "right" mate for each and every one of us. This kind of meeting is more than just physical attraction, more than camaraderie or a comfortable at-home feeling when you are with the other person. Soul mate conjunctions are born of fire and thunder, and a tangible, sweet calm pervades the atmosphere whenever the two finally bond. Friends, family and strangers see it—this magical aura that cocoons the lovers. It is the thing that protects the soul mates from harm and keeps them together. Is it a blessing from God? Definitely. Is it earned somehow in this lifetime or a past lifetime? Who knows. But the real question is, how do I know if I've met my soul mate?

The story of Jenni and Brad has miraculous signs staked all around them. If you are angelically aware, you'll see them.

Jenni is a very dear friend of mine who lives in Houston. She is a single mother, making it on her own like many others.

But despite hardships and pain, Jenni has a light inside her that barrels up from her soul like a steamroller and bursts through her blazing brown eyes and constant, brilliant smile. She is beautiful on the outside, yes, but she's even more wondrous on the inside.

Last December Jenni drove to Austin from Houston to attend to a speeding ticket she'd received weeks earlier. She had her two-year-old daughter in the car, and they had no more than gotten on the road to make it to Austin for her court date, when the worst snow and ice storm in years struck.

The fact that it was snowing in nearly subtropical Texas is strange in itself. Commonly, December brings snow to the panhandle of our great state, but for us in Houston, it's rare. Therefore, we are not accustomed to driving on ice. Jenni's two-hour trip turned into four hours. Her daughter, sensing her mother's tension, was afraid as well. By the time she got to Austin and dropped her daughter off at her mother's house, Jenni's nerves were frayed.

To make matters even worse, Jenni finally got to the court-house on time and found a note on the door that court had been canceled due to inclement weather. Now those frayed nerves split in a hundred different directions. She felt as if she'd risked her life and that of her only child's for nothing.

Jenni decided she wanted to calm down before going back to her mother's, so she stopped at Hudson's on the Bend. This is an obscure, out of the way, elegant restaurant and not patronized by the happy-hour crowd. In other words, the place was nearly empty when Jenni walked in. There is a huge fire-place and lovely tables in cozy, peaceful surroundings. It was just what Jenni needed.

As Jenni tells it, there were only seven people in the entire restaurant due to the ice storm. As she ordered some dinner and a glass of wine, she noticed a particularly handsome man about her age, sitting across the room from her. From time to time as she would look up, she would see him glance her way. She smiled, but then looked away. The man began staring at her so intensely that he made her nervous. She wasn't afraid of him, nor did she think he was strange, but she got the distinct feeling that he wanted to speak to her. She told herself that she was a single woman, and she was perfectly within social boundaries to go up and speak to him, but she lost her courage. Finally, a male friend of hers joined her for dinner. They finished their meal, and as she left, Jenni thought to herself, "Gosh, I hope that guy doesn't think that Eric is my boyfriend. He's just a friend." Within seconds she stopped herself again, thinking, "I'm losing my mind! I will never see that guy again. And after all, we only looked at each other across a room."

Christmas came and went. The New Year was ushered in. February rolled around and so did Jenni's rescheduled court date for her speeding ticket.

Back to Austin she drove. For the second time, her court date was rescheduled. Once again, her day was not going well. On this particular evening she had arranged to meet a man she had been dating at a funky Asian restaurant in an old house with stars and moons adorning the red walls, called Mars.

She was ushered to a table, knowing that her date was due to arrive any moment. Suddenly, her cellular phone rang and her date, who was in Dallas, stated that the weather had turned ugly and that his flight had been canceled. He was not going to make their dinner date. It was the perfectly bad ending to a perfectly bad day.

Instead of leaving, she decided to simply order dinner. She was half-finished with her meal when a very handsome man was seated only two tables away from her. He pulled out his cellular phone, Palm Pilot and a book. She assessed that he was intentionally alone, whereas she had been stood up.

The man glanced at her, smiled and then looked at her again. She smiled back, knowing from his demeanor that he wanted to speak with her. Finally, he asked, "What did you order?"

The ice was broken. He asked her to join him at his table. He ordered dinner, and they began talking. Their conversation flowed easily, as if they'd known each other all their lives or had been fast friends and had just found each other again.

At one point, Jenni went to the ladies' room. While in the bathroom, she looked at her reflection in the mirror and thought to herself, "This could be the guy for me. This feels so right." Then she stopped herself.

"That's crazy! I just met him! What am I thinking?"

But as she started out the door she stopped herself and said, "But you never know."

Rather than being afraid of her natural intuitions and feelings, she had the courage to allow these thoughts to rest comfortably inside her, like a bird coming home to the nest.

They talked all night, at least until they closed the restaurant. Brad said to Jenni, "I'm not ready to have this end. Would you join me for a drink at the Four Seasons?"

Uncharacteristically, Jenni not only agreed, but she got into his car with him. This action was something Jenni absolutely, positively never, ever does. She amazed herself at how at ease she was with Brad. They shared more conversation and a drink. Then Brad drove her back to her car where they said their good-byes.

"You know, Jenni," Brad said, "I don't get to Lakeway that much. But I know a wonderful place where we could go next time I'm here and you're here. It's called Hudson's on the Bend."

"It's one of my favorites!" Jenni exclaimed.

"I haven't been there for the longest time . . . not since, well, the ice storm back in December."

In that split second they both stared wide-eyed at each other. Goose bumps enveloped Jenni as Brad said, nearly in shock, "That was you! You wore a red sweater and black leather pants."

"It was me, Brad," Jenni said.

For the next two weeks, Brad telephoned Jenni every day. They found their likes, dislikes and goals were on an even parallel. Finally, after two weeks they had their actual first date.

Author's Note: May 2005. This story took place years ago. Today Jenni and Brad have been married for several years and now live in Austin. Their lives couldn't be happier.

Fortunately for them, their awareness of life is a bit more keen than most and a bit more grateful. They know their extraordinary journey to find each other was not coincidence, not a fluke. They are proof that when heaven intervenes in the mortal world, ours is not to question. It is to accept, live and love.

The Great Flood, Part 1

n spring 2001, I promised to pick up a friend who was flying in from overseas at five o'clock in the morning at Houston's George Bush Intercontinental Airport.

As a general rule when doing this, I have a habit of setting three alarm clocks and then lie in bed with one eye open just knowing that those clocks aren't going to work. By the time I finally get up at four to walk the doggies, start a pot of coffee and get dressed, I'm exhausted. I have done this for years and I would like to think that by now I have moved into the groove on this, but I haven't.

Because I'm so worried about anyone who travels on those long international flights, or any flight for that matter, it never, ever occurs to me to worry about myself or what is going on down here below.

This particular time, while I was pretending to sleep, watching the clock, Houston experienced a torrential rainstorm. We'd been having a great deal of rain that entire spring, due to the weather systems of La Niña and El Niño, which had dried up Texas like a skeleton of tumbleweed, but this rainfall was more than severe. I was to discover later that it was a killing storm. It was the night of the century's worst flood in Houston. Little did I realize that within hours newscasters would deem it "The Great Flood."

That morning I was fully aware of the pounding rain, thunder and lightning enough to phone the airport to inquire if it was still open. When I finally got through, I discovered that planes were indeed landing, and not only that, but my friend Alan's flight was twenty minutes early!

I grabbed the golf umbrella and walked the dogs out to the street for a quick "tinkle," then raced with them back to the garage where they jumped into the back of my Tahoe.

With a hot tumbler of coffee in my hand, we set out on our journey. I shut the garage door with the electric opener, never giving a thought to the fact that I had not checked the weather report on the weather channel. My friend was arriving early, and I had to get to that airport.

From my house in the Galleria area, it's a quick hop up onto the 610 South Loop. As I drove through the rainy streets, I thought to myself how very dark everything was at that hour of the morning. In fact, it was so dark, I couldn't even see the grass and flowers on the side of the road.

"It's always darkest before the dawn" went through my mind.

I told myself there was some natural explanation as to why it was so pitch black. Must be something with the earth's angle, the rising sun. The setting moon. That had to be it.

I got up to the Loop and headed north for a few miles before I veered off from the 290 interchange at I-10, which ran east and west, and then took the 610 North Loop.

Pelting rain kept me from going too fast, which gave me time to realize there was an inordinate number of cars parked along the shoulders of the freeway. My first thought was that they had parked last night during the worst of the storm. Because I'd been half awake all night long, I was aware of how forceful the wind and rain had been at points in time.

Peering into the parked cars, however, I noticed that most had been abandoned. I thought nothing more of it and continued on.

In the back of the Tahoe I always put the long bench seat down and keep one captain's chair up for Beau, the oldest Golden Retriever. He likes to sit where he can watch people out the window. Bebe always rides with her front paws on the console between the driver and passenger. That way she can watch what's coming from the driver's perspective. Junior, the eighteen-month-old, walks around from window to window and usually watches the passing cars and scenery out the back. He's sort of my "border patrol." All three are terrified of thunder. I've seen Beau lift all fours completely off the ground if it's a big enough boomer. He is old enough and sharp enough to know that when lightning streaks across the sky, he'd better brace for the noise. If he could, he'd put his paws over his ears.

This gives you a good idea of what I had going on inside the Tahoe as we drove another ten miles or so to the junction at I-45 North and South. My route is to continue on 610 East through the spaghetti bowl of ramps and exits for I-45 onto the Hardy Toll Road and then out to the airport.

I was surprised at the number of cars and trucks on all the freeways this early on a Saturday morning. Just as we were coming up to the junction I noticed that all the cars were slowing down.

"Not an accident!" I said aloud, easing up on the gas.

The rain was still coming down. Again I noticed how extremely black everything seemed. I slowed the Tahoe to nearly a standstill. As I peered out of the front windshield I saw that the cars were completely stopped on both I-45 North and South. Next, the cars in the eastbound lanes of 610 had stopped. Rather than pulling up behind anyone, I veered off to the left and stopped in the painted triangle that separates the lanes at 610 and the I-45 North ramp.

"This isn't right. Something is wrong," I said to myself.

Bebe nuzzled my neck. Then she froze on point. Her eagle eyes saw something moving.

I squinted into the blackness.

Up ahead I saw not one, or two, but four or five people open their doors and literally jump out of their cars. They raced to the I-45 northbound ramp, ran up the embankments and pavement, and then I saw them hang over the railing as if looking down on something.

"What in the world is going on?" I was mystified.

My nature is never, ever to turn back. My nature is to either sit very patiently and wait for traffic to clear or to find a way to keep going forward.

Suddenly, it was as if time stood still. All three dogs sensed danger. They stopped panting.

In my head, I could almost hear them talking to me. Like doggie telepathy.

"Mom, we can't stay here. Go home."

My thoughts at that second were that even if there was some terrible accident, I could never get to the airport on time. Also, it would be cruel of me to make the dogs sit in the car for a half hour or hour or longer without food or water.

I had absolutely no clue whatsoever what was going on up ahead, but my instincts kicked in, and I decided to turn around and go back.

My greatest, all-time, number one fear of all fears has always been that I would find myself in a situation in which I was forced to drive down the freeway going the wrong direction facing oncoming traffic. As clichèd as the "freeway car chase" is in movies, it scares the living daylights out of me to watch those scenes. I positively never wanted to be John Candy driving the wrong way with some semitruck coming at me in a rainstorm.

Well, at that moment, that's exactly what was happening. As I turned the Tahoe around, two other cars decided to follow my lead. Why they would do this, I didn't know.

"They must be as crazy as I am. Or maybe they have dogs in the car with them, too."

I turned on my hazard lights and inched my way down the shoulder.

Cars came at me, honking, waving me back, rolling down their windows and cursing me. Giving me the finger. I didn't care. White-knuckled, I clung to that steering wheel and kept going. My heart was racing a mile a minute. I have never been that terrified in my life. (Well, maybe when the armed robber stuck a gun to my forehead and told me he was going to kill me, I've been that scared. But that's another story.)

For miles, I drove against the abusive rain and oncoming traffic.

It was too much for the woman in the car directly behind me. She stopped her car and parked on the shoulder. She couldn't go on. The next car back wove around her and followed me.

Finally, I got to a point where 290 and 610 South feed onto 610 East. Here, I had to cross over six lanes of traffic in order to get up onto a different section of highway.

Terrified, I panicked. I stopped my car. I burst into tears. I couldn't do it. I couldn't get home.

The dogs were scared, too, I knew. I could feel their tension. They could feel mine.

At that moment, the itsy-bitsy compact car behind me wove around me. I could see a young man waving at me to follow him. He was young, I thought. He didn't know better. It wasn't that he had more courage; it was that he didn't realize the precariousness of the situation.

But right then, I needed his naïveté to lead us. His lack of knowledge just might save us. I followed him across all the lanes, darting in and around the oncoming cars who blared their horns at us both.

But we made it!

Driving up the far left shoulder, we slowly crept onto the single-lane on-ramp. Now we faced a single file of half a dozen cars, lights blinding us as we forced them to let us exit the freeway.

Again they honked their horns and shouted at us.

We circled around under the freeway and for the first time in over a half hour, I was finally driving in the correct direction in the correct lane.

I breathed easier.

At the next light, I turned right onto the street that would lead me home. The young man in the compact went straight. I waved at him and he gave me the high sign as we parted company, strangers in the night, yet forever bonded because of our ordeal.

"Doggies, that young man was an angel," I said. "Thank you, God, for bringing him to me when I needed him."

I drove home and got to the house just as the phone was ringing. I knew it was my friend.

"Hey, I'm here!" he said.

"Well, I'm not there, and I don't think I'm coming. Something terrible has happened."

I grabbed the remote control for the television and turned on the news. I was shocked to see aerial photographs of the intersection where I'd just been. It was completely under water. The semitrucks that had passed me were floating down 610 and I-10.

"What's going on?" he asked.

"The city is immobile. We're flooded everywhere. I couldn't get through. I don't know what made me turn around and come home, but I just had a feeling that something awful was happening."

"I can tell you there is something going on. I'm walking through the airport, and there must be thousands of people here. They are sleeping on the floors . . . and the monitors say that . . . oh, my God! All the flights have been canceled."

"The television is showing everything now. It's a nightmare out there. Now I can see why it was so black all around me. It wasn't that it was dark. It was that it was all water up around and over the freeways!"

"Don't worry about me. I'm glad you are home and safe."

"Me, too."

We hung up, and as I watched television that morning, I couldn't believe what I was seeing. At predawn the newscasters were already calling the flood the worst in Houston's more than 150-year history. By noon, it was declared a federal disaster area. The Red Cross was out in full force. National media now referred to it as "The Great Flood."

At five o'clock in the afternoon I watched an interview with a truck driver who had been forced to "swim for his life." To my astonishment, I realized he was talking about the exact same place I'd been twelve hours earlier.

"This wasn't just floodwaters," the truck driver said. "The water came rushing at us like a wall. One minute I was passing around cars and the next, my trailer and I were floating. I rolled down my window and jumped out in time to swim to safety. I had wondered why all of a sudden cars had slowed to a halt. I had seen people jumping out of their cars and then running up the exit and on-ramps, hanging over the railings. I wished I would have had the good sense to turn around, but that was impossible with a big rig like mine. I did see a few SUVs and cars turn around and face the oncoming traffic."

My eyes bugged out of my head as I watched that man on television. "That was me he saw!" I said aloud to the dogs.

They looked up at me, and all three smiled in that way that only Golden Retrievers can. It was as if they were saying, "We know, Mom. We were the ones who told you to turn around."

"Thanks," I said and hugged them all.

I was reminded of the research I did for *Wings of Destiny,* my historical novel about the 1906 earthquake in San Francisco. For hours before the great quake, horses whinnied, dogs barked, cocks crowed and coyotes in the hills bayed, sounding an early alarm, but few listened.

Perhaps it was that research that saved our lives the night of the Great Flood. My memory banks could have kicked in somewhere back in that obscure vault, alerting me to my own animal instincts. Maybe it was mental telepathy from my pets. Also, it could have been an angel on my shoulder whispering in my ear.

All I know is that we escaped imminent disaster, and I will always be grateful.

The Great Flood, Part 2

he Saturday morning of the Great Flood in Houston, Texas, my friend Alan walked out of the International terminal thinking he'd find a shuttle bus to take him to the main terminal. Instead, he found the normally jam-packed loading and unloading docks empty.

"This is like a ghost town," he said, scratching his head. There were no taxis, no buses, no Park 'N Fly shuttles, no passenger cars, limos. Nothing. His only choice was to walk to the main terminal, which he did.

By this time, the rain had subsided. At the airport the sun was peeking out from behind the canopy of clouds. Alan entered the terminal from the baggage claim area doors, and as he stepped inside he was stunned.

"This looks like a World War II movie scene!"

Lying on the floor, in the chairs, up against the baggage carousels were not hundreds, but thousands of sleeping people. It was only five-thirty in the morning; therefore, most people were still sleeping. Babes in arms, students, entire tour groups were just beginning to rouse.

The impact of the scene drove home to Alan the seriousness of the situation. What I had told him on the phone was not an exaggeration.

"This city is immobile," I had said.

Making his way through the terminal, he finally found a television tuned to the news broadcast.

"George Bush Intercontinental Airport has been home to over six thousand stranded passengers last night due to Tropical Storm Allison. Officials at the airport state they are already running low on food and water. Transportation out of the terminal is nonexistent. All outbound flights are canceled, though planes are still landing, bringing thousands more to the city with no way of exiting the area."

Alan was still in disbelief. "I can't stay here. There's got to be a way out."

Alan rode the escalator to the main floor hoping that the Continental President's Club was still open. He called me from his cellular. "If there's no food or water in the main terminal, maybe the President's Club will still have some."

"Alan, try to get some rest. They are saying on television you could be there for days!"

"I did not fly all this way to stay in an airport!"

"Alan, let's be realistic. No one can get to you."

"I'll figure it out."

The President's Club was still open, and he eventually found a vacant chair. He called his friend on the north side of Houston, thinking if he could make it to the Woodlands, he could then work his way home. At least he'd have a shower and clean bed for the next few days until the city dried out. However, his friend was flooded in. He could not get out of his street.

Alan called me and asked me to see if I could find Giles, a favorite cab driver. I called Giles, and he said, "Miss

Catherine, my house is flooded! I'm trying to save my family. Pray for us!"

Hanging up, I did just that. In fact, as the news worsened and story after story became horrific, I, like many Houstonians, prayed and prayed some more.

By eleven in the morning, Alan was frustrated, tired and hungry. He still was adamant about trying to get to his home. A hopeless hope.

Finally, he made the decision that he was going to try one more time to make it to town. He still believed there would be a cab. Outside the terminal doors were nearly five hundred people all looking for a cab. Alan's hope deflated.

He overheard some of the passengers saying that every twenty minutes to half an hour a cab would make it through. There still were no buses or shuttles. Still no passenger cars.

His hope puffed up again.

"If I don't find a cab in the next hour, I'm going to rent a locker, stow my hanging bag, and I'm going to walk home." Alan was resolved.

At that moment a taxi drove up.

Like a swarm of locusts, the crowd descended upon the lonely cab. People shouted their destinations. The cab driver turned them all down.

The driver got out of the cab as more people begged for information about the city and about the condition of their destinations. His answer was always the same. "Sorry. Impassable. I can't get there."

The crowd dispersed, waiting for another taxi. Hoping against their hopes.

Alan stood off to the side, knowing that his vision of walking twenty-five miles to home was going to become a reality.

The cab driver left his taxi and walked straight up to Alan.

"You want to go to the Galleria, don't you, sir?"

"Why, yes!" Alan replied.

"I can take you there."

"How is that possible? You just turned down all these people."

"I just got a radio report from a buddy of mine. He made it through by going north of the city westbound on FM 1960 to 290 South and then . . ."

". . . straight to nearly my backyard in the Galleria!"

The cabbie smiled. "Yes, sir. That's about the size of it."

Alan slapped the man on the back. "You have just made yourself a lot of money."

"Let's do it!"

Ironically, the route that brought Alan home entailed some of the same strip of freeway on which I had, only hours earlier, been forced to drive *against* the oncoming traffic! Because 290 is elevated almost entirely from the north side of the city into the Galleria area, little or none of it was affected by the floodwaters.

As Alan drove over the devastation, acres of flooded subdivisions, retail centers and freeways, he was brought near to tears. He could see people still standing on bridges and overpasses, looking down on their abandoned cars and homes.

"I've been to war, and that's so different, but this . . . I can hardly believe this is happening."

Alan arrived home safe and sound. Later that afternoon, Alan came over, and we learned how close to death I had come. The newscaster stated that the great deal of flooding that had caused the "wall of water" to race toward my Tahoe on the freeway had been caused when the International Ship Channel had backed up and flooded Buffalo Bayou, which connects to the Channel and then flows out into the Gulf of Mexico.

For the next days, even weeks, we watched the devastation of our city. Blessedly, where I lived was in a high enough area that my house was not affected; however, I had nowhere to go. It took days for the roads to become passable again, just for a few blocks. Communications were nonexistent. Calls were not allowed into the city. Power was off. Over twenty people were eventually found dead.

One of the things I have always admired and loved about Houston is the people. The willingness of the citizens of my city to help each other is astounding. Heroes were made in those days of danger, the likes of which I may never witness again. Ordinary citizens revved up their boats and paddled canoes, rescuing others from rooftops. The stories of strangers jumping into rushing waters to pull men, women and children out of sinking cars and trucks were commonplace.

A *Houston Chronicle* photographer, exhausted from taking photos all night long, finally started home through pitch-black streets when his motor died in the hubcap-high waters. Stepping out of his SUV, the water rushed him and torrents pulled him into a drainage ditch where he was neck deep, struggling for life for over an hour. A passerby drove up, took out a ski rope from his pickup and pulled him out of the water. To profuse thank-yous, the savior simply said, "You would have done the same thing for me, wouldn't you?" Then he vanished.

Angel? Or human? In a crisis, what difference does it make?

That same story was repeated thousands of times. Even as Hermann, Methodist and St. Luke's Episcopal hospitals shut down due to lack of electricity because of the flooding, and the patients were flown to surrounding area hospitals, we were all glued to our television sets, watching silently, impotently, while nature concluded its devastation of our city.

The chaos was staggering, yet at the same time, I watched a news crew from Channel 13 fly an emergency mission from one end of the city to save the life of a patient undergoing transplant surgery. Privately owned helicopters joined in the "life-lift force," bringing so many to safety. Children were plucked out of trees and off rooftops. Pets were saved from drowning by total strangers who then called the networks, placing bulletins about the animals' locations. Just as much care was taken to reunite pets with their owners as families with each other. Over six hundred cats and dogs were admitted to the Society for the Prevention of Cruelty to Animals in the wake of the storm. The staff worked seven-day weeks and staffed the phones for twenty-four hours daily until the crisis abated. Each time I saw a pet rescued, I thought of my own three Golden Retrievers and how torn I would be if anything happened to them. The response of Houstonians even to our pets made my heart swell with happiness, pride and hope.

Downtown was inundated. At 5:20 A.M. on June 9, the waters of Halls Bayou had crested at ninety-one feet, thirteen feet above the one-hundred-year floodplain. Four billion dollars worth of damage ensued.

One man dove under the water to retrieve his daughter's suitcases out of the trunk of her car. When he got below the water he found a semitruck sitting on top of his daughter's car.

A woman died when her elevator hit the bottom floor, opened, and she drowned. The final death toll was twenty-two.

In the next few days as the waters receded, food drives, clothing drives, furniture drives, you-name-it-to-help drives became our lives.

One of the messages the angels have given me and others is that we are put on earth to serve God by helping people. Sometimes I think natural disasters occur only to give us that chance to help someone else. That is what I saw during the Great Flood. Neighbors saving neighbors. Strangers saving lives of strangers.

Through it all, everyone prayed. And our prayers were answered.

Even a month later, we were still digging out and drying out. We were still waiting for the power to come back on and for our lives to come together again. Downtown parking garages and buildings remained flooded. Houses were ruined; people were living in shelters or with friends, unable to return home.

Today, many houses have been rebuilt. The offices have reclaimed, freeways fixed and new bridges built. Houstonians will never forget the night of the Great Flood. We will never forget the multitude of angels who flocked together, saving us, our children and our pets.

It was a night when human beings were the answer to their own prayers.

Angelic Visitations

he stories in this section pertain to those visitations that occur while a person is awake. These occurrences involve an angel appearing in human form only. If an onlooker were to witness a visitation, there would be nothing out of the human realm of experience to report. These angels do not have wings. They are dressed in whatever the current fashion or mode of dress is for the country and culture in which they manifest. They speak in the known dialect and language of that country or tribe. Their very existence at the moment of their visitation is purposely fashioned *not* to bring attention to themselves. They are about the work.

These are not stories about "apparitions," in which an angel appears to a person, giving a message. The apparition does not actually interact with the person or perform any kind of physical work or healing. I would like to take a moment to explain "apparitions."

Most of us have heard stories in which an angel, resplendent in white gowns and with enormous wings, appears to a holy person, saint or prophet. There are many of this kind of angel story in the Bible. For the most part, we feel disconnected with those ancient times when people seemed to have a better chance at being visited by an angel than we do in contemporary times. Or do we?

About fifteen years ago, I met a woman, Kathy Gillian (not her real name), in Houston, Texas. At the time, she was a fairly prominent psychic in Houston. She worked at a day spa not far from where I worked in the pool industry. Kathy had been interviewed by the leading local newspapers and had been on several television shows. Today, in 2005, that doesn't seem all that odd, especially considering the popularity of cable television shows such as *The Medium* and *Pet Psychic.*

I had gone to Kathy's apartment to consult about a charity event we were both hosting. I asked her if she had ever seen an angel. She told me that when she was only four or five years old she had been playing in her bedroom. She saw a bright light, and when she looked up from her dolls, the walls and ceiling of her room had simply disappeared. It was as if dense matter had transformed to ethereal light and energy. The angel was very tall, blond, blue-eyed and wore white robes and a white gown. It had a gold rope belt around its waist. Kathy said she couldn't tell if the angel was male or female, because it felt like both. (This kind of reporting is why I always refer to this kind of angel as androgynous.)

She was not ill at the time. She was not in any danger at all. The angel had come to tell her that she was not alone and would never be alone. She was to understand that God loved her and that her life would be a very special one. She would always "see" things that other people did not. She was to have patience with other humans who could not "see" or understand what she would see.

When Kathy was an adult, she had been revisited by her angel only a handful of times, but she did feel that the angel spoke to her and through her each time she gave guidance to one of her clients. She never felt disconnected from her angel, and it was a constant source of comfort, hope and love.

As simple as this apparition story is, it has stayed with me all these years.

In this "angelic visitation" section, by contrast, the stories are true interactions with an angel. Most times when this type of interaction takes place, humans are either in danger of their lives or are in such great despair and hopelessness that angelic intervention is necessary.

From the stories submitted to me, I have established a criterion for this kind of "angelic visitation."

1. The angel, in human form, appears seemingly out of nowhere.
2. The angel is a total stranger.
3. The angel vanishes into thin air moments after the "life-saving" moment or the danger has passed; or at the very least, he or she is never heard from or seen again, as if that person didn't exist.

I was in a meeting in Los Angeles recently discussing this book and my previous book, *Angel Watch.* One of the producers in the meeting told me a very interesting story about his interaction with an angel. He was not in danger at the time, though he was questioning things in his life.

The angel appeared to the producer as a well-dressed man in his forties at the Boston airport during a particularly bad snowstorm. All the flights had been canceled. Passengers were scrambling for hotel rooms and places to stay. Everything was booked. The weather forecasters predicted that the storm would last for days. There would be no buses or trains out of town, either.

The producer and his wife had no place to go. They were lamenting their situation when the man sitting next to them at their gate offered to take them home with him to his house and put them up for the duration of the storm, assuming they could still get out of the airport. Not knowing how long the blizzard would last, the producer and his wife agreed to go home with the man.

The man, or rather, the angel, took them to a pleasant street with small but nice homes. For two days the producer and his wife stayed with the man, shared meals together, cooked together, played cards and watched television. When the airport reopened, the man ordered a cab for the producer and his wife to take them back to the airport. The man had canceled his business trip, however, making his own return to the airport unnecessary.

The producer and his wife were about two miles from the man's house when the producer's wife remembered that she had left her nightgown in the bathroom. The cab driver turned around and drove back to the man's house.

When they arrived at the proper address they found the house not only locked and vacant, but the front window had been boarded up.

The cab driver double-checked the address and his directions. He had not made a mistake.

Not believing what had happened to them, the producer went to the next-door neighbors' house and asked about the house that was boarded up. The neighbor stated that the house had been abandoned for years and that the property was involved in a very strange estate situation. No one had come to claim the house or sell it. Everyone in the neighborhood thought the house was very strange.

The producer, his wife and the cab driver left that day, knowing that they had been paid a very special visit. It was the producer's wife who claimed that the man was an angel because at each meal the angel had made a special request to say the "blessing" over their food. His blessing had been quite loving and deeply felt. The producer had to agree with his wife.

And the cab driver?

The producer never got his name or his cab number in order to check on the man's reactions or his further corroboration of this story.

To this day, the producer isn't quite sure if the cab driver was human or angel.

As fantastical and strange as some of these stories may sound, I believe that in addition to the obvious need for the angel's appearance and interaction with the human in question during times of danger or need, these wonderful situations happen to make us aware that angels truly do live and walk among us.

Dallas Angel

AUTHOR'S NOTE: *This story was told to me by a reader whom I met at a Barnes and Noble book signing in Fort Worth in June 2001.*

Melanie was driving around a warehouse section of Dallas looking for a particular discount house a friend had told her about. Thinking about all the bargains she was going to scoop up, Melanie had her mind on merchandise and not on the directions she'd been given.

Sure enough, she got lost.

She circled around the block again, still looking for a particular address when, suddenly, she blew a tire. She got out of the car, inspected the tire and realized the car was now inoperable. She needed a tow truck.

Outside the protective metal of her automobile, Melanie looked at her surroundings with new eyes. She realized that she was in a very dangerous part of town. She had no cellular phone. She had no change for a pay phone. She was stranded. Isolated. Vulnerable.

On the corner at the far end of the block, a group of boys in their late teens or early twenties clustered together. Smoking cigarettes, listening to a boom box, they had heard the blowout.

They watched her at first with curiosity.

Melanie saw one of them say something to one of the other boys. He laughed uproariously. Then the one who'd been slouched against the building stood. He eyed her from head to foot.

The sun was going down. Darkness crept over the buildings like a death shroud.

Fear pricked the hairs on the back of her neck. Sweat sprouted across her forehead. Her hands went clammy. Her heart raced. Glancing up the street and then down, she saw no other cars about. There were no other people, only these boys.

Every alarm in her body sounded.

Danger.

Instinctively, Melanie only knew of one thing to do. She said a prayer. "God, help me."

At that instant, seemingly out of nowhere, a van appeared, and a middle-aged man hopped out. He slammed the door of the van very hard as if making a point. As he rounded the front of the van, she realized he wore priestly clothing and a white collar.

"You need some help, honey?" He asked with a jovial grin.

"Yes. Yes, I do," she replied, her words sticking nervously to the edge of her tongue.

"I don't have a jack myself, otherwise I'd fix it. Jump in. There's a station near here. We'll find some help."

"Oh, thank you!" Melanie said as the minister gently took her by the arm, opened the door to the passenger's side of his van and helped her in.

"Yep. We'll get you rollin' in a jiffy!"

The minister climbed into the van, started the engine and drove past the street gang as if to defy their power.

They turned a corner, then another, then another and found a brand-spanking-new gas station.

"Why, they're so close!"

"You just gotta know where to look!" the minister said gleefully.

Melanie and the minister got out and went up to the pit crew who were taking a break.

"This young lady desperately needs your help, gentlemen."

"Sure," the older man said. "What's the trouble?"

"I have a flat tire. I forgot the name of the street, but it's only three blocks from here," Melanie said.

Turning, she said, "Do you remember where . . . ?"

The minister was gone.

"Where is he?" she asked.

The man lighting his cigarette glanced up. "Oh, the pastor? Why he's right . . ."

"What the heck?" The older man stepped around Melanie. "Where's his van?"

"Hey, what gives? How could that guy leave so fast?" the man with the cigarette asked.

Melanie smiled to herself. "Because he wasn't a man. He was an angel."

The two men gaped at each other, scratched their heads and agreed. "My kind of angel."

Shine

have known and loved my friend Cherry for nearly twenty years. She and I have been through just about every trial, tribulation, joy and triumph that two friends could ever know together. We have a bond that's pretty darn invincible. We've been through illnesses together, divorces, birth of grandchildren and deaths. She even is the human mama to one of my Bebe and Beau's puppies, Copper, whom she named after her own Copper who died several years ago. To say that Cherry and I are like sisters is an understatement.

However, in all these years, until two days ago, I never knew that Cherry had a deceased sister, Shine. Why this information had never come out, I don't know.

Whenever I think of Cherry—tall, blond and green-eyed beauty that she is—I always think of a glowing white light around her. Of all the people I know, even in my dreams, Cherry comes to me as a white orb. She just "shines."

You can imagine how surprised I was when I realized that perhaps this shining white light could be her sister on the Other Side.

Shine was the opposite of Cherry in looks. Shine had brown hair, brown eyes and an olive complexion. She was born five years before Cherry. Cherry's father, Chad, had been home only a few months after World War II when the family moved to Texas from Kentucky where Cherry's mother, Cyd, and Shine had been living.

Shine barely knew her father since he was off to war most of her very young life. However, she was a bright child, full of enthusiasm and imagination. She was always kind to everyone, never knowing a stranger. She loved to dance and sing and make up songs. In fact, she even made a record. She loved performing in front of an audience whether they were family, friends or strangers. Shine was, indeed, special.

From an early age, Shine told her mother about her "imaginary friends." Because Chad was away from home so much, Cyd indulged her young daughter in her fantasies. Rather than stifling her creativity, Cyd allowed Shine to talk about her "friends."

Many were the times when Shine and Cyd set an extra place setting for "Dr. Smith." Shine would interpret Dr. Smith's conversation for her mother. Admittedly, Cyd thought that because Shine's father was absent, her daughter needed to fill that void with another male presence. Her "invention" of Dr. Smith somehow made sense.

Sometimes Shine would come into Cyd's room at night and ask her mother if they could all sleep together. Of course, they had to make room for "Dr. Smith." However, once the war ended and Chad was home, Cyd expected Dr. Smith to vanish.

He did not.

Instead, Shine's stories about her friends became more exaggerated, or so she thought.

One day when Shine was five years old, she was playing in

the backyard while Cyd, three months pregnant with Cherry, was washing dishes.

"Mama! Mama!" Shine called as she raced across the yard and into the kitchen.

"What is it?" Cyd asked looking up from the dishpan.

"I just saw God."

"What? Where?"

"In the backyard!"

Cyd dried her hands and asked Shine to sit down. She smoothed her dark hair and gazed into her daughter's eyes. No falsity there. "What did he look like?"

"I didn't see all of him. Only his hand."

"Why on earth would God be reaching down to our yard?"

Shine swallowed hard. "Because, Mama, he came to tell me that he wanted me to come with him."

"Where?"

"To heaven."

Chills shot down Cyd's spine. She grabbed Shine to her chest. "Don't say such a thing, darlin'."

"But Mama, it was God. He's wonderful." Shine pulled away from Cyd. "Are you crying?"

Turning her eyes away from Shine, Cyd replied, "No, of course not. That would be silly. Now, you run along and play."

Cyd went back to the dishes as Shine left the kitchen. Her hands were frozen. Something told Cyd this was no ordinary imagination her daughter possessed. Still, the idea of Shine dying was impossible. The girl was not sick and had never been sick. She was healthy, energetic and happy. Nothing was going to happen to her daughter. Not if she could help it.

"I just have to be extra cautious and make sure she doesn't

get hurt playing. I'll watch her more closely. She'll be fine. She'll be fine. She has to be."

Within two weeks Shine contracted encephalitis and died a week later. Just as Shine had predicted, God reached his hand down from heaven to bring her "home."

Cherry was born six months after Shine's funeral. To this very day, Cherry believes that her sister has been with her always. Though they never "knew" each other in this life, they are one in spirit.

Fireplug Angel

suppose there are some people who never go through "starving artist syndrome," as I call it. It's one of the reasons I held myself back from committing to my divine path for a long time. Being a literature and history major in college, I was too aware of the biographies of Hemingway and others like him who lived on nothing but rotted apples and pigeons they'd slingshotted to death in the Jardin des Tuileries in Paris. Sounds exotic and romantic, but in real life, it's the pits.

I was at the lowest point in my life, or so I thought at the time. Though I was home in Indiana and worked with my sister and mother, the rest of my life was in despair. I missed my son. I missed my girlfriends in Houston. I missed the dreaded city traffic, the smell of Mexican food and the taste of icy margaritas. I missed the bookstores where I used to hang out with my friends who worked there. I missed the profusion of azaleas in spring and the sound of the gardener's blowers and weed trimmers I'd detested when I lived there. I missed muggy, hot days that made my makeup slide off my face, and I missed the sound of strangers saying, "How're y'all doin'?" I missed Texas. Period.

On weekends I wrote ceaselessly, hoping a publisher would pick up one of my novels. Just because one has been published does not ensure employment. Publishers merge and lay off writers and editors. Publishers go bankrupt. Editors leave. There are all kinds of things that happen in publishing.

Writers write. Without a contract, we then become working, starving artists. That's the hole I was in. Plenty of stories to tell, but no contract.

Where I was living was, for me, as depressing as life could be. The converted garage where I had my computer and files was not insulated or well heated. In fact, it was freezing in there. Out of one window I gazed at a rusting trailer dumped off in a neighbor's yard, and across the street was a water tower, its paint cracked and peeling against the merciless midwestern winter.

Soot from the Gary Steel Mills clung in the air, crystallized into gray snowflakes and coated the windows. I felt a kinship to Dickens, who lived in mid-nineteenth-century England during the industrial revolution and wrote of such depressing scenes.

Even worse, there was an invisible, negative hopelessness that embraced the town I was in like an evil embryonic sheath, threatening to come alive and strangle anyone who dared escape its snare.

If I'd contracted a life-threatening disease, I would have mustered the energy to battle it, but this insidious discouragement was worse. Depression implies a nonactive force. This was not depression. It was akin to frustration, constantly gnawing, whittling away at my self-esteem, my belief in my talent and my trust in my divine path.

"If God wanted me to be a writer, then why don't I have a paycheck for that work?"

Simple reasoning, right? So I thought.

My psyche was at low ebb when I lumbered to bed one night in May. Little did I realize that the angels would visit both my sister and me, living in two separate towns, and my life would make an about-face.

I dreamed I was lying on a gurney in a hospital operating room. A team of doctors was working on me. I could hear them talking, and though I was numb from head to toe, I was awake during the operation.

I remembered thinking, "This is some great kind of local anesthetic!"

The head doctor, the one with a light attachment on his head, looked up from my midsection. "She's dying."

"I disagree, doctor," a female voice replied. "Check the blood flow."

The head doctor moved to my arm and sliced it open. I felt nothing. "No blood."

I was shocked. "What do you mean no blood?"

"There's no blood in your veins, Cathy."

"How can that be? I'm alive!"

The female doctor clucked her tongue. "Barely alive."

"Yes, I'm afraid it's true," the head doctor said. "You see? The blood has turned to powder. Pink powder. Not even red at that."

"Why has this happened to me?" I was truly panicked.

"No emotions," the head doctor said.

"No will to live," the female doctor chimed in.

"So that's it? I just dried up?" I was aghast.

They began gathering up their tools. "We can run a few more tests, if you wish."

"I do wish!" I protested. "I . . . I can live. I'll show you," I screamed as they wheeled me out of the operating room.

I woke up at that moment drenched in sweat, my heart racing to beat the band. I felt my arms, legs, midsection. I was all in one piece.

I looked out the bedroom window at the water tower. It had lost even more paint over the winter. The paint had turned to powder, just like my blood.

"I'm not doing this anymore! I hate it here! I've got to get my life back on track!"

I shot out of bed, dressing in a flash to get to work at Nan's shop. Just as I was dashing out the door, the phone rang. It was Nan.

"Cath, I had the strangest dream last night. I dreamed you were dying."

"What?" Goose bumps skewered my flesh. "That's impossible. I had the same dream!"

"You went to the Tribunal?" Nan exclaimed.

This was a new take for me. *Tribunal?* I'd read about people dying and coming back, and when they were on the Other Side, they faced a "judgment board" of "light beings." There were always three or five beings in number. Dressed in white robes, these male-type angels or beings discussed the person's life with him or her. Whereas I had had the privilege to meet Jesus (see "Death Becomes an Angel") many people go before this "board."

However, Nancy did not read the same kind of books I did. She was immersed in financial guidance, small-business advice books and biographies of successful entrepreneurs.

After running her shop six days a week, ten hours a day, raising three children and helping Dave with his dental practice, not to mention her seat on the Tourism Board, Chamber of Commerce and church work, the last thing Nan had time for was any other kind of reading.

I was fairly certain she had no prior knowledge of such spiritual judges. Therefore, there was nothing in her memory banks to "cloud" the issue.

"Nan, this Tribunal, who were they?"

"There were three men dressed in flowing white robes with white hoods. They were very old, with white hair and white beards. They sat behind a very tall desk just like a judge in a court. They said they were there to take you to heaven. I was there pleading for your life. I had ahold of your hand, and I said, 'She's my sister, and I won't let her go. I'm not going to let you have her.'"

They said, "She wants to come here."

Nan continued. "They called themselves 'The Tribunal,' that's how I'm supposed to refer to them."

"That's accurate, Nan. I've read about these beings and this board."

"You're kidding! Then this wasn't a dream? I was really there?"

"It's possible."

"You know, it was so real. So intense. I felt like I was there. It's still just so clear, I can't explain it."

"So what was the verdict?" I finally asked.

"They said you decided you didn't want to come to heaven." She paused a minute. "So, Cath. Are you moving back to Texas?"

I nearly dropped the receiver. "How did you know?"

"I just know."

"I . . . I didn't know until this morning that I have to move. I have to go. I really will die if I stay here. I'm miserable here."

"Then you should go."

I drove the forty-minute drive from my house to La Porte, through scenic, rolling Indiana hills. As much as I love that part of the country, it was where my home used to be as a child. It wasn't my adult home.

I got to the shop, and my mother intercepted me. "Come on," she grabbed my hand.

"Where are we going?"

"Late breakfast. Early lunch. Take your pick."

We went to a nearby restaurant. After being served a cup of coffee, Mother said, "I've never seen you this unhappy. What's it going to take to get you to move back to Texas?"

"I need a thousand dollars for a U-Haul."

Mother reached right down in her purse and pulled out her checkbook and wrote out a check.

"Mom," I stared at the check with tears in my eyes.

"Don't say anything. Are you sure that's enough? I don't have much, but I can . . ."

"Mom, I can figure it out. I'll line up a job before I go. I think Shelby will rent me her beach house for next to nothing. I've got my computer and plenty of paper. Ryan and Christy are building their new house and haven't a stick of furniture. I'll give them everything I've got. They need it—I don't. That saves me storage on things and then, well, God will just have to show me the way."

"And he will," Mother said.

That night I called my friend Shelby in Houston and asked her when her beach house was coming available. Unfortunately, it was already rented for the entire summer. I wouldn't be able to rent it until October.

"Catherine, when do you want to move back?" Shelby asked.

"Right after my Book Expo Convention, which is June third."

"That's only two weeks from now. How very interesting," she mused.

"What's interesting?"

"I have a boarder who rents my daughter's old room in my house. Would you be interested in that?"

"I've never rented just a room before. How strange. I'd just told mother this morning that I wanted to give all my furniture to Ryan and Christy for their new house they've just moved into. All they have is the few things from their college apartment. I have a desk, chair, computer and clothes."

"That's all you need to come live with me!"

"Shelby, you are an angel. A real answer to my prayers!"

"You'll be my angel. I have to have surgery on my neck in July. If you'll help nurse me through that, I'll let you have the room."

"It's a deal!"

Over the following two weeks I packed my boxes, stored my books in the attic of Nancy's shop, went to the Book Expo and packed the U-Haul. I hired a friend of Nancy's to drive my little red car behind the U-Haul to Houston. I would drive the truck.

On the morning we packed my twenty-two-foot yellow Ryder truck, Dick and Marti Davis were my angels. Nancy and I had been packing everything the wrong way. Dick had once earned money as a mover and knew exactly how to position the furniture and items. We finished in four hours. I made arrangements to spend that first night at Mother's house, and then I would start on the road back to Texas the next day.

I drove out of the subdivision where I'd lived for the past year, feeling the grip of hopelessness that still clung to the area like smoke. I had absolutely no regrets about leaving this part of my life behind.

About a block from the country road that led to the highway, I saw a boy sitting on top of a fire hydrant.

He was an unusual-looking child, one I did not remember seeing in the area before. He was so pale-skinned and light-haired, he looked like an albino. He was thin to the point of emaciation. His cheeks were sunken and he had dark circles around his eyes. He was dressed in a tattered old athletic-type T-shirt that hung on his bony shoulders and a pair of shorts. No shoes.

I was struck with that old vision of mine of the starving urchins from the London streets in Dickens's *A Christmas Carol.* In the movie version, the Ghost of Christmas Present lifted his robes, and clinging to his legs were starving children.

Oddly, many times I'd referred to friends and others about my life at that time being Dickensian. Looking at the urchin on the fire hydrant blasted that notion home to me.

I pulled up to the stop sign, looking straight ahead at the boy on the opposite side of the street off to my right.

Slowly, he smiled at me.

I smiled back.

He raised his hand and gave me a triumphant "thumbs-up."

I gave him a thumbs-up, back.

"That's right!" I exclaimed. "I'm outta here!"

"You're outta here!" he shouted back.

I drove forward, still giving him my thumbs-up when I realized he couldn't possibly have heard what I said. Yet he'd distinctly yelled, "You're outta here!" to me.

I glanced back in my rearview mirror to see if he was following me, or if he was still giving me the high sign.

The boy had vanished.

Not two seconds had passed from the time I'd seen him out of the truck's passenger-side window and the time I had glanced in the rearview mirror.

Clearly, he was nowhere to be seen.

That little angel had come to tell me that I was on my divine path, that as terrifying as it was to face a new life with no real job in place, not even an apartment of my own, everything was going to be okay. Everything was just as it should be.

My life was going to turn out just fine.

All I had to do was to have faith.

Clare and the Bedside Angel

AUTHOR'S NOTE: *This story is from Jim Keating.*

y wife, Clare, was once told by a psychic that a beautiful blond woman would appear at the foot of her bed. For a very long time, this apparition did not occur, and we had put the prediction out of our minds.

Then about four years later, in the early morning light, she saw the woman by her bed as foretold. It must be stated that Clare was not asleep, but wide awake, when this woman came to her.

The surprising thing was that the woman was still living, though she was a great distance away. She was someone Clare knew and had felt guilty for offending many years before.

The woman appeared from the waist up and had wisps of golden light flowing from her in the same manner as dry ice. The golden light and her presence gave a complete and utter feeling of love and forgiveness to Clare. It was mystifying that it was someone still on the physical plane, yet it was comforting that such a degree of forgiveness was expressed.

To this day we both wonder over the soul's ability to travel out of the body. Perhaps this woman knew how deeply sorry Clare was and she, in her loving heart, reached out to Clare, like a prayer.

Perhaps it is true that our prayers are always answered . . . one way or another.

Andrew's Mystery Man

host or angel?

Now, that is a good question, isn't it? How does one know if the person who mysteriously appears in the middle of the night in the back hallway of a supposedly haunted house is a ghost or an angel?

I have my own theory on this dilemma. I believe that if the spirit simply manifests to make his presence known or felt, then it is a ghost. *A ghost has personal ego.* It is their personality, their need to remain on, near or attached to this earth that makes them ghosts, or at least those vaporous spirits we refer to as ghosts.

An angel can appear in human form out of thin air, then vanish before our very eyes. An angel, however, comes to this plane for a specific purpose. Usually an angel is here to save a life.

My friend Vicki's son, Andrew, was in college when he was confronted with this question.

Andrew was on his way home from his summer job one night. It was just past twilight on a country road, and he was dog-tired. Approaching a train crossing, there were no cars in sight. The cross arms weren't lowered to stop traffic; no warning bells rang and no lights were flashing. As he drove up to the crossing, Andrew naturally assumed the coast was clear.

His headlights shining straight ahead, he continued forward, his mind consumed with thoughts of a hot shower and evening meal. As his music played on the radio, he did not hear anything out of the ordinary.

Just as the front end of his car was nearly to the tracks, a man appeared out of nowhere, standing on the tracks.

Andrew immediately slammed on the brakes, rocking the car to an instant halt.

The man stared at Andrew.

How did he get here? Andrew stared back. He blinked. He hadn't seen the man run up, walk up or drop out of the sky.

Clearly, the man "appeared."

In less than a second, a loud horn sounded and a long train came speeding down the tracks right in front of Andrew.

Dazed, Andrew expected to see the man's remains splattered over his windshield and front end, but as he peered closely at the window, there was no blood. No body parts. No clothing scraps.

The train zoomed past and left a wake of darkness behind.

Still, the cross arms did not descend. The lights never flashed. The warning bells never rang.

There was literally no trace of the man to be seen.

Andrew immediately got out of his car, carefully checking to see that no other train was coming. The tracks were whistle clean. No one had died there that night.

Scanning the surrounding countryside and roads, Andrew saw no trace of the man. He called out to the man, but no one answered.

Goose bumps enveloped Andrew as he got back in the car. His hands were shaking as he gripped the steering wheel. It was all he could do to make himself turn the key and start the engine again.

"This just doesn't happen to me. Things like this don't happen!" he said to himself.

Slowly, Andrew eased the car over the tracks and down the familiar road he traveled every morning and night to and from work. Still, he saw no one on the shoulder walking away.

Trying to make sense of the impossible is difficult for most people, but Andrew is not most people. Since he was a small boy, his mother had told him of everyday miracles that had happened to her and her family all their lives.

Driving away, Andrew said to himself, "There is no mystery to that man. He was my guardian angel."

Andrew lifted his eyes to the bright night stars. "Thanks," he said. "Thanks for saving my life, angel."

Angelic Miracles

he musical *Flower Drum Song* contains a wonderful song packed with a spiritual message I have never forgotten. The lyric is "one hundred million miracles are happening every day."

These miracles are part of life and living, true. They are the flowers and grass that bloom every spring without fail. The gestation and birth of a child is a momentous miracle, especially for the woman carrying the child.

However, angelic miracles are those tiny incidents that probably don't mean much to the person standing next to you in the supermarket line, or your brother or best friend, but in their way, they light your life path for you like runway lights on an airstrip. When these "signs" occur, you suddenly grasp the answer to a question that has been plaguing you. When these little miracles take place, your life can change in the twinkling of an eye.

Have you ever been in a situation at work where you found yourself surrounded by coworkers who seemed to undermine your every move? Perhaps there was a particular person who made your life miserable. He or she stole your ideas, took credit when it was due to you or perhaps even took your job.

Suddenly, the boss calls you on the carpet. You are terrified. You need this job. Your livelihood and that of your family depends on this money. You love your work, just not the people you are dealing with at this point.

You approach the boss. You just know he's about to fire you. You say a very quick prayer as he begins his litany of complaints about you. From some deep well inside you, you find courage you didn't know you had. You can't believe the words coming from your own mouth. You have power and strength of conviction you've never felt. You state your case in such a manner and use words you didn't even know you knew.

Your boss is stunned—happily. He is able now, as a good manager, to see both sides of the equation before him. Now that you have stated your case, he can make an accurate assessment. He thanks you for your input. He respects you and values your opinions as never before. You have greater self-confidence.

A month later when promotions are announced, you are promoted; or perhaps you are not promoted, but you receive a bonus or raise you had not expected, which alters your opinion of yourself. For the first time, you *dare* to dream of a different career course for yourself. You *dare* to think and even plan for something better for yourself. Perhaps a few seminars, night classes, even college would help you get a better job. You start thinking outside the parameters that you have drawn for your life.

That moment back there in your boss's office was an angelic intervention. Your angels had come to your rescue by giving you the words to say that would alter your situation. They infused you with strength. They filled you with courage just as if you were a warrior on a battlefield.

That miracle moment was spectacular, perhaps even

life-altering for you. Did your boss see it? No. Did the rest of your coworkers feel any kind of alteration in their lives or careers? No.

Even your nemesis would not have recognized anything unusual. Because this enemy was the energy behind the conflict coming about, he might be aware of the portent of the outcome of your meeting. He might be fearful that he will be caught in his lies. Delusional, manipulative people do not care about others nor would they recognize strength, courage or an angelic moment. They only look out for themselves.

I do not believe in "coincidences" or "accidents." I don't believe the universe is chaos. If you look closely you can see that the universe is God's perfect thought. Every aspect of it is infused with love. With unconditional love there can only be order, beauty and perfection. There is abundance for all.

The universe can be chaos if you choose disruption. If you make a "drama" out of everything that happens to you, you will keep attracting negativity and negative, life-disturbing incidents to you. You will spend your life going in circles and never accomplishing your goals, and you will make everyone around you miserable.

"Coincidences" are brief minutes in time and space where the human and the divine intersect to create an angelic miracle. You should drop your jaw in awe. You should open your eyes and truly see the wonder of the moment. You should give thanks to God and the angels for making this positive action on your behalf. Once you begin to acknowledge these little miracles in your life, it is amazing how many more you will experience, until the point when you realize that your entire day, month, year and life is divinely led. These angelic moments can be the result of a departed loved one who is "helping" you from the Other Side, or they can be divine intervention. They occur to prove to you that you are never alone. You are never without angelic first aid.

Gerry's Joke

My friend Gerry died on December 16, 1998. Few people knew that Gerry was ill, because Gerry was a proud man, and he just could not make himself actually say the words, "I'm dying," to any of us.

The day Gerry died in New Orleans, I got the call from his wife, Darma. I promised her that I would come to the funeral. I flew to New Orleans and attended the services and the graveside burial as well. It was a devastating time for Darma because she had not seen the signs of Gerry's cancer.

I had only known Gerry for a year, not decades. From the moment I first met him, I saw his yellowed eyes and instantly suspected that he had pancreatic cancer. Unfortunately, I had not known Gerry when he was healthy and fun-loving and full of the promise of life. I had also only known him in illness. However, in that short time, I felt that we had made a real connection, on a deeply mental and spiritual level. At least that was my interpretation. I didn't really know for certain at the time of his death if we had bonded as much as I intuited that we did.

A year after Gerry's death, in February 1999, I was scheduled to attend the NATPE (National Association of

Television Producers and Executives) convention, which was held yearly in New Orleans. (Today it is held in Las Vegas.)

I had lived in New Orleans for three years beginning when my son was only fourteen months old, from 1973 to 1977. We owned a little white brick house on the river side of Veteran's Memorial Highway in Metairie. I had fond memories of days I'd take my toddler son to the French Quarter, just the two of us, and we'd comb through the antique shops, and I'd buy him pralines for the trip home. We listened to jazz musicians in Jackson Square and dropped coins in their black top hats. In the winters we'd go to the flea market down by the old cotton warehouse district where I sold my dried flower arrangements and fabric wreaths while Ryan sat on the old railway curb chewing on sugarcane stalks.

New Orleans was home to us in those years; therefore, I knew my way around the city pretty well. It is also one of those cities like San Francisco that seems timeless. Though it tries to spread out, and new buildings scrape the sky, its romantic essence remains.

I arranged with my cousin's daughter, Sonja, to stay with her and her husband, Bob Berle, and their brand-new daughter, Lila. I was thrilled to see Sonja again. It seemed like aeons since her fabulous wedding to Bob, only three years prior. The fact that I would be there when Lila was only a few weeks old was a bonus.

Sonja and Bob lived in a historical house they were renovating in the Garden District. When she gave me the address and directions, in my mind I knew precisely where to go.

After landing at the airport, I rented a car and took a city road map, just in case I did get lost, and set off. I called Sonja from my cell phone and told her I shouldn't be more than half an hour. I'd be in time for supper that evening.

It is a straight shot down I-10 to the Garden District exit I knew I was to take. Coming in from the west I was reminded of my days in New Orleans. I drove past the mall where I used to shop. I even saw the exit I used to take that led to my little Metairie house. Because of the late hour, however, I didn't have time to take any side trips down memory lane. I wanted to see Sonja and Bob and couldn't wait to hold Lila in my arms.

Still cruising down I-10 I watched for the exits.

"Boy, they sure have a lot of new exits off this freeway," I said to myself, as late afternoon traffic began stuffing the lanes.

I turned the radio to a local jazz station and kept driving. I passed downtown and suddenly, I felt those strange goose bumps climbing up my back.

"This doesn't look right," I said to myself, taking out the city map. More traffic kept me from actually pulling over to examine the map. I kept driving, and as I did, I knew I was far past the Garden District.

I took an exit and found myself dumped into a spaghetti bowl of twisted city streets. I had not a clue where I was.

It took me twenty minutes to figure out how to even get back on the freeway and head back west to find that Garden District exit.

Two more turns and exits, and I was gratefully back on I-10 headed back the way I had come.

Settling back in the car, I knew I wouldn't miss my exit.

However, the strangest thing happened. As if in the

twinkling of an eye, in half the time it took to get lost, I had not only come all the way in from the east side, but had passed through downtown and was now far, far out in Metairie all over again!

I couldn't believe it. This was my old stomping ground! How could I, who truly do possess a good sense of direction, get so confused? I got off the freeway, made a U-turn and started back in again.

For the second time coming in from the west, I knew I wouldn't miss that exit. It was clearly marked, that I knew for certain. After all, nearly half the tourists coming to New Orleans either exit to the Garden District or French Quarter.

Lo and behold, I found myself back downtown again. I had passed the French Quarter exit!

Banging my palm on the steering wheel, I berated myself for stupidity, blindness and carelessness.

I exited again, made yet another U-turn and headed west to retrace my tracks again. This time I knew not to drive quite so far.

I told myself that years of living in Houston, the fourth-largest city in the United States, was making me misjudge my distance. New Orleans is tightly confined.

I looked up and saw an exit, "Metairie Park." I remembered that exit somehow, but couldn't quite put my finger on when or why I was there.

"I'm taking it!" I said to myself, throwing the map down on the seat.

The second I turned left under the bridge of the freeway and stopped at the stoplight I suddenly knew the reason I'd gotten lost.

"Gerry! You old devil, you. Or angel."

Directly in front of me was the cemetery where Gerry was buried! Only a year earlier I had been at this cemetery for the one and only time in my life at Gerry's funeral.

"Okay, Gerry, you win!"

Rather than head in to the Garden District, I drove straight. I circled the cemetery twice waving at the headstones, trees and angel statues. "Hello, Gerry!" I said with the window rolled down.

"I know you can hear me! I know you are having fun with your little joke on me! Just as I know you will now help me find my way to Sonja's house and take care of me during my trip here to New Orleans."

I said some prayers for Gerry that afternoon and for all his family, children and grandchildren.

I realized several things that day.

The first was that, somehow when being divinely or spiritually contacted, it is quite possible to lose a sense of time and distance. One moment my trip had seemed to take forever. When I turned around, the distance seemed minute, as if I'd flown over the space rather than driven it in my car.

The second was that if I'd ever had any doubt about my own bond and friendship with Gerry, it was put to rest now. I had come into Gerry's life at a time when he was dying. He didn't know how to tell his wife or his friends about his cancer, and so he had "arranged," even in life, to have me do it for him.

I had been quite aware of the symptoms of pancreatic cancer because a neighbor of mine many years ago had passed away from this disease. Gerry had been diagnosed two months before I met him.

I think Gerry's spirit or consciousness knew this about me. Gerry never asked me directly to intercede for him; perhaps it was an unconscious thought that I intercepted on some heart-string kind of telepathy. Maybe Gerry's own angels told my angels to tell me all this in a dream. I'll never really know. Well, actually, like all things, I'll know when I, too, cross to the Other Side.

Because Gerry always, even to the end, possessed an eccentric sense of humor, I believe his little joke that day in New Orleans was his way of saying, "Thanks for being there for me, Cath."

I love you, too, Gerry. I always will.

Ray Meets an Angel

ay Ebberman has been a friend of mine for nearly a decade. As an architect and interior designer, Ray has become more than just the creative artist that helped to transform my Houston house from blueprints into an elegant and romantic retreat from the world; Ray is family.

Ray was living in San Francisco when his son, Raymond, died suddenly. Because Raymond was only nineteen, and his illness had not advanced to a life-threatening stage, Raymond's passing was nearly impossible for Ray to accept.

Grieving over the loss of his son sent Ray into a deep depression. Because his heart was bleeding, and because I loved Ray so much, I invited him to come to Houston for a long visit.

For days, I trolled antique shops with Ray where he let his creative genius run untethered. I introduced Ray to my friends Vicki and Wendy and filled him with all the Cajun seafood he could manage. We sat in air-conditioned wine bars laughing at jokes and sharing stories. We did everything, except talk about Raymond.

On Sunday morning, I cooked a big Southern breakfast, minus the grits, since only my mother can make decent grits in our family, and prepared to take Beau and Bebe for their hour-long Sunday stroll.

Ray took me aside. "Cat, instead of walking with you and the dogs, would it be all right with you if I went to church instead?"

I looked into his misting eyes and saw his pain. "You should be in church, Ray. It's important. I have a feeling you'll find some answers there."

"I hope so."

"You will, Ray. It will be a revelation."

I gave Ray the directions to my Catholic church, St. Michael's. He took my Tahoe while I set out for Tanglewood Boulevard with Beau and Bebe. It was a beautiful day, and I got lost in the many conversations I had with friends I met on the Boulevard.

When I got back home, Ray had not returned. I checked the clock. Mass had been over for better than half an hour. Since the church was only a few blocks away, I knew it was impossible for him to have been lost. I worried that perhaps the electronic remote on the security gate to my complex was not working. I went outside, and at just that moment I saw my car pulling up, and Ray was beaming.

He parked the car in the garage while I waited at the back door.

Ray looked as if he was walking on air. And he had been crying.

"Cat, you won't believe what happened to me today."

"Come sit in the living room and tell me."

Ray was so choked up, he could hardly talk. I made us some tea while he gathered his thoughts.

"This is the most fantastic thing I've ever lived through."

"Start at the beginning, Ray," I said.

"You know all about Raymond's death, but what you don't know is that I have felt so terribly guilty as if I was the cause of his death."

"No, Ray . . ."

"Hear me out," he said.

"I was in Boca Raton when I got the offer in San Francisco. Raymond had been in Boca as well. While I was there it was easy for me to check on him, fix supper for him, take care of him. Then I was transferred to San Francisco. I had to take the job or lose the job I had. So, I moved. Raymond wanted to come live with me, but it was impossible right then. I was in an interim apartment, still trying to move my things from storage in Boca to storage in San Francisco. I wanted him with me, but the timing was wrong.

"Only days later, I got the call that Raymond had suffered a seizure and had died. It was all over so fast. All I could remember were his last words, 'Dad, I want to live with you.'"

My heart split apart for Ray and his pain, but the look in his eyes was filled with joy. Something had happened. Something drastic. I let Ray continue.

"Today at church, I was praying for Raymond. Praying for myself. You know that part of the Mass where the priest asks everyone to turn around and shake the hand of someone behind or next to them? Well, I turned around and there staring at me was a young man who was the spitting image of Raymond.

"I felt my blood turn to ice, but I shook his hand. I said, 'Hi, my name is Ray.'

"The young man said, 'Hi, I'm Adam. I just moved here to come live with my Dad.'

"Adam turned to his father. 'Dad. This is Ray.'"

It was my turn to be enveloped by the chills that tell us divine intervention is at hand. "Ray, this is just an amazing . . ."

"Miracle!" Ray blurted. "It was nothing short of a miracle. That boy had come to Houston to live with his dad. It was as if Raymond was saying to me, 'Dad, I'm here with you now, and you'll never be without me.'"

"That's right, Ray. That's exactly what was happening. I mean, what are the chances of you being in that particular church on this particular day when a boy who just happens to look exactly like your son, just happens to go to the same Mass of which there are five any given Sunday to attend, and just happens to sit right smack behind you and just happens to have moved to Houston for the reason of wanting to live with his dad?"

"I feel as if the weight of the world has been lifted from my shoulders, Cat. I haven't felt this light, this loved in ages! I feel as if . . ."

"You could go on with your life?" I concluded for him.

"That's exactly right. I know now that no matter where I go, whatever I do, I can talk to Raymond as if he's standing in the same room," Ray said, happiness radiating from his face.

"I think another thing Raymond is trying to say to you, Ray, is that just because he's dead doesn't mean you're supposed to stop loving him. When you think of it that way, love is truly eternal."

It's been eight years since this incident happened to Ray. He's been through some tough times and a great deal of spiritual healing and evolving. He's moved from San Francisco back to his hometown of Biloxi, Mississippi, via a stint in Houston. He's with his family again and is now the very proud grandfather of two granddaughters. He's closer to his daughter than he would have dreamed possible back in those dark days after Raymond's death. His business is thriving, and his career is showering him with one creative project after another. During a recent phone call from Ray, he told me that his life had never been so filled with joy, so peaceful, so fulfilling.

Would anyone think it could be less? After all, Ray has his son with him to lead him home.

Vegetables at the Mailboxes

obody ever really wants to talk about failure. When you think about it, it's the one thing we should discuss, because everybody fails at something at one time or another. It's from our failures that we learn how to do things right. Failures show the way to the right answers.

Edison failed over a thousand times before he made that lightbulb work. Colonel Sanders was turned down over a thousand times when he was struggling to sell his Kentucky Fried Chicken.

It's that blasted human pride that makes us want to shove failures under the carpet, pretend they never happened and lie to ourselves a bit longer that we are just a bit more successful than others.

It's also failures that lead us straight down an angelic highway.

It was a rotten summer for me. Just as it was for my friend, Alan. Plain old rotten. After a year of struggling to get a new business off the ground, Alan's business partner and financial backer pulled out. He wanted more immediate results and wasn't getting them. Being an entrepreneur, Alan has explained to me, means working five times harder and longer than anyone else and taking at least a hundred more risks on a weekly basis.

I have since revised this statement. It means gambling everything in your life, including sleep and meals, to make a dream come true. You have to have nerves of steel, the courage of a gladiator, the faith of Job and a lot of Pepto-Bismol to be an entrepreneur. To be friends with one, you have to have a sense of humor, even *more* faith, and a half cup of insanity doesn't hurt.

All this considered, I was limping along financially on a smattering of royalty checks, hoping for the phone call about a new book deal. All the while I prayed that I wouldn't get sick, and that went for my Golden Retriever, Beau, as well.

The Houston summer heat sweltered man and beast. My air-conditioning bills were a scandal. The pantry got bare, but somehow I kept the phones going.

I told no one of my situation. It was too embarrassing. I didn't want my friends, family or my son to know. I surely didn't want my mother to know. I remembered thinking, how would I ever keep my head up if the neighbors knew? I told myself it was temporary. In time, this too would pass.

But it didn't. May moved into June. Then into July. Then into August. My wits were unraveling. My discouragement was tangible. It infested my life like locust-devouring hope.

I lied to friends when they asked me to go to dinner with them. I didn't want anyone to know my failure. My pride wouldn't let me.

I hid my tears, knowing that even my angels weren't seeing me cry anymore. Somehow, I felt as though I had been abandoned, but I didn't know why.

One afternoon, I had been writing a particularly emotional scene for a novel, and Alan called me.

"Would it be all right if I came over and got Beau and took him for a walk down to the mailboxes to get the mail?"

"Sure," I replied. *Why bother? It's just going to be a bunch of bills I can't pay.*

"I just want to get out of the house for a second," he said.

"Sure, get out of the house," I repeated. I've always thought little exchanges like this were stupid when I heard them. Like I was going to go somewhere. Where? I couldn't even put gas in the car.

It was that day that I realized that humans say these inane things to each other for reassurance. We don't say stupid stuff to inform. We say it to give comfort.

"I'll put Beau's leash on him and meet you at the front door."

Alan rang the bell and took Beau for his walk.

I wrote another paragraph and just as I had hit the return key, I heard the front door bang open so hard the wall upstairs shook.

"Catherine, come quick! Come quick!" Alan yelled at the top of his lungs.

His voice was so urgent, I knew something had happened. Terrified, I bolted from my chair.

"What is it? Is it Beau? Is he hurt?" I raced down the hall and to the stairs.

"No, it's not Beau," Alan yelled.

"Are you okay?" I was yelling as I took the stairs at rocket speed.

"I'm . . ."

"You're what?" I demanded as I turned the corner around the little kitchen and stood in the dining area looking at Alan standing in the doorway, the sun at his back, Beau wagging his tail next to Alan and smiling at me as if he'd just caught a squirrel.

"It's a miracle!"

"Alan?"

His voice was more full of tears than his eyes.

And his arms . . .

His arms were filled to overflowing with all kinds of vegetables.

"A miracle, I tell you!" he said, shutting the door with his foot.

"What is all this?" I went to him as he handed me a half dozen tomatoes and juggled a watermelon in his arm.

"Squash, potatoes, eggplants! Melons! Look at all this stuff!"

"Alan, what in the name of God . . . "

"That's just it. There is all this food at the mailboxes and there was a sign. 'We have too much food. Please take some.'"

"No way." I was dumbfounded.

"Go down there and see for yourself. Bring back some onions. You could make a salad or fry up some tomatoes, and look!" He held up an eggplant. "What can you make with this?"

"A feast! Is . . . all." Now I was crying. "It's an answer to a prayer."

"I know. Now hurry."

I practically flew out the door. Sure enough, there was the sign, just as Alan had said. Though I thought he had taken too much at first, I couldn't believe how much was left. I was reminded of that Bible story about the fishes and the loaves.

Was this stuff self-generating?

From the bushel basket I plucked more tomatoes, onions, green beans and zucchini. My mouth was watering, my stomach groaned, and my eyes filled with tears.

"Thank you, God. Thank you, Angels. Whoever you are."

I, too, filled my arms with so much food I thought it would take weeks to eat it.

When I got home I was shaking. Alan was already washing vegetables.

When we sat down to dinner that night, our thanksgiving was so profound, so heartfelt, we both knew words were inadequate. We closed our eyes, held hands and let our hearts do the talking to God.

Then we dug in.

Our stomachs stretched to bursting, we sat back and discovered the serving dishes were still full.

In all my life before and since, there has never been a thanksgiving meal like that one. The bounty at the mailboxes did not come from an angelic spirit. It was from Ilene Robinson and her husband, who had a ranch in west Texas. They had brought the food that, if it had been left on their ranch, would have rotted in the Texas heat. They had been my angels when I needed them.

To this day, they probably still do not know how much we needed that food on that day, because the real miracle came the following morning.

The next morning I went to the mailboxes and found a large check from my publisher and a contract for a new novel from another publisher. In the twinkling of an eye, I was caught up on all my past due bills and paid my rent in advance. Beau got his favorite treats he'd been missing, and I stocked the pantry once again.

My prayers of thanksgiving have never stopped. Today I am in the position to be an "angel" for others, and it's wonderful, but it all started with some vegetables at the mailboxes.

Sally in Paris

We all know what fun it is to go to a new city, resort or nature area where we've never been. We can pretend we are explorers of the unknown, and as long as our adventures don't take us too far from civilization and a hot meal, we pretty much do all right.

When dealing with the unfamiliar we tend to go a bit slower, stop along the way to read the historical markers, or make observations about the topography, wildlife or architecture we've never seen. The thrill of discovery is what travel is all about.

Imagine, then, a fourteen-year-old girl flying overseas for the first time. Her heart would be fluttering at the mere mention of Paris. London. Rome. She might scour the library and travel bookstores for information. Today that same girl would log on and download bits and pieces about popular cafés, shops, guided tours and tourist attractions.

When Sally was fourteen she accompanied her parents to Paris for a two-week vacation. Though her parents had been to Paris, Sally only had photographs of the Eiffel Tower, Arc de Triomphe and Champs-Elysées in her memory banks.

For weeks she practiced her travel-guide French phrases, made lists of the women's couture shops she wanted to hit and counted out her allowance, wondering how long it would last in an expensive city like Paris.

The family landed at Orly Airport and took a cab to their hotel on the Rue de Montaigne. From the second Sally walked through the airport terminal hearing everyone speaking French, she felt as if she'd come home. The inflection of their voices, the raspy laughter of men who smoked too many cigarettes and even the discourtesy of the gendarmes at the exits were eerily familiar to her.

"Even the air is different in Paris," Sally told me as she related this story to me. "There is no question the lighting is different in Paris. It's as if the sunlight is filtered through some kind of pink-tinted lens, making every leaf and flower seem more romantic, more alive than anywhere else. There is an energy that embraces you in Paris. Despite how gruff the waiters are, how much some Parisians, not all, appear to dislike Americans, I never saw it. I experienced only people who looked at me with loving eyes as if I was . . . well, family."

The hotel was old and charming and small. The staff was sweet, and though proper, they seemed pleased to have such a young American residing in their hotel. This in turn made young Sally feel special.

Once in their rooms, Sally opened her suitcases and began unpacking. Carefully, she hung her clothes in the closet. She laid out her pajamas and underwear in the drawer. When she went to the bathroom she was not surprised to find two toilets. "Oh, the bidet," she said aloud to herself, walked away and stopped dead still.

"What did I call that?" She clamped her hand over her mouth.

"A . . . bidet. That's what I said." Goose bumps rained down her arms.

She shook her head. "I must have read that somewhere. Or mother told me."

She finished unpacking and then went next door to her parents' room.

"When we finish unpacking," Sally's mother said, "I want to find something small, quaint for a quick bite to eat."

Sally had gone toward the window and pulled back the draperies. Without looking outside, she said, "There's a café around the corner. Let's go there."

Sally's mother looked up. Assuming Sally had spied something out the window she replied, "Fine."

How did I know that? Sally wondered fleetingly to herself. Then she glanced outside, and seeing no immediate café on the block, she brushed the entire incident aside. *Must be the jet lag mother warned me about. We can ask at the front desk about a restaurant. Paris is famous for its food. It won't be hard.*

The trio left their rooms and walked out into the sunshine.

"Which way?" her father asked.

"This way," Sally replied without thinking and taking off to the left. "Toward the Eiffel Tower," she continued and pointed at the looming famous iron structure.

"I forgot how magnificent it is," Sally's mother said.

"Me, too," Sally said walking in front of them. Suddenly, she stopped. *What am I doing? I don't know where I'm going.* "Dad, maybe we should ask at the desk."

"I thought you saw a restaurant."

At that moment, a strange confidence filled her. "I think so. Maybe I was wrong."

"No matter," he answered. "There's bound to be something close."

They continued on, window-shopping along the way. "Could we go to Harry Winston's after lunch?" Sally asked. "It's only a few blocks away. Down that way. Behind us." Again, she pointed in the correct direction.

"How did you know where Harry Winston's was?" her father asked.

Shrugging her shoulders, Sally said, "I must have read it."

"Oh," he replied with an assured nod.

Just as they were about to turn the corner, Sally was filled with that strange "knowing." In her mind's eye she envisioned a café. "It's the café with the red awning and white stripes. The food is really good there. Especially the pan au chocolat," Sally said feeling particularly hungry at this point.

"Sally?" her mother began as they turned the corner.

Two doors down a red and white striped awning protruded over a small café with tables and chairs sitting outside on the sidewalk.

"I don't remember ever coming here before," Sally's father said.

"We haven't," her mother replied, her voice turning cautious.

They sat at a round table and a waiter promptly appeared.

"Bonjour," he said taking out a pad and pencil. "Vous êtes Américainês, n'est-ce pas?"

"Oui," Sally replied. "Je m'appelle, Sally."

"Very good, Darling!" Sally's mother said.

"Pan au chocolat et lait pour moi, s'il vous plaît," Sally smiled at the waiter.

"Oui. Et vous?" He looked at Sally's stunned parents.

"Darling, you're speaking with a perfectly natural accent. Did you pick that up on your tapes?"

"What tapes?"

"Why, your language tapes."

"I read a book," Sally replied matter-of-factly.

Clearly the waiter not only understood English, he was impressed. "Young mademoiselle has perfect inflection," he offered with admiration.

"Merci," Sally grinned widely.

They placed the rest of their order and in the middle of lunch without thinking, Sally said, "Mother, there's a shop near here that sells pretty china boxes. Can we go look at them?"

"You mean Limoges, dear."

"I don't know what they're called. I just want to see them."

Assuming this was another place Sally had read about in a book, her mother agreed they would go shopping before heading to Notre Dame.

The family finished lunch, left the café and started down the street. Window-shopping and chatting along the way, all were mindless about their destination when Sally suddenly looked up and saw the street sign. "The shop is on this street!"

Picking up her pace, Sally whisked away ahead of her parents. She was a block away and already looking in the shop window at dozens of antique Limoges boxes when her parents caught up to her. "See, Mother. They're very special. One of a kind."

"Why, I've never seen boxes like this. These must be very old."

"And very expensive," Sally's father rolled his eyes.

As they entered the shop Sally had the overwhelming impression she had been to this particular shop before. Everything about it was familiar in some way. The tin embossed ceiling, the old bronze chandelier, the hundred-year-old cabinetry that held the fabled Limoges boxes.

"I feel like I've been here before," Sally whispered to her mother.

"That's impossible, dear. You've never been to Paris. You're just having déjà vu."

"Déjà vu?"

"Yes, it's the feeling you're feeling. Like you've been here before. Scientists think it's a slip in time. That you simply moved ahead of yourself a fraction of a second, or rather that your mind did. Then when you walked in the door, you've seen this place before."

Sally peered at her considering this explanation. "No. That's not how I feel. It was different when I knew it. The walls were gray. Not blue. The floor was wood . . . squares."

"Parquet," her mother corrected.

"Yes, but not this carpet. It smelled different then."

Sally lost interest in the boxes, though her mother lingered over the beautiful workmanship. Sally felt an eerie sensation flood her. The longer she remained, the more about the place's past came back to her.

"It's like I lived here before," she mumbled to herself.

Finally, they left and began their walking tour of the city. From the Eiffel Tower to Notre Dame, they took it all in. They walked along the Seine, gazing at the river and crossed back and forth over the bridges, buying trinkets from the souvenir stalls. Sally spent an abnormally long period of time inspecting the original paintings by unknown and obviously poor artists. She herself possessed a gift for painting, and anything to do with art of any kind intrigued her.

However, throughout that first day and every day to follow, no matter where they went, Sally felt she knew every inch of the city. Nothing seemed new to her. Every tree, flower, building and café was familiar, like old friends with whom you never lose touch.

Near the Sorbonne and the University District where the oldest sections of the city still remain, Sally was enveloped with chills. It was here she could nearly describe every single building, she knew every block.

"Sally how much did you read about Paris?" her father asked. "I wish you took this much interest in your social studies classes."

Sally's mouth was dry, and her hands were shaking as she gazed at the buildings around her. "I . . . I don't know what's happening to me. I didn't read about any of this. Sure, I knew about the Eiffel Tower and the Arc and what the outside of Notre Dame was like, but I tell you, I don't understand. I don't even know my own school as well as I know this city. And the shops. How did I know where that Limoges shop was? There are hundreds of such stores in Paris. But that particular one? And the perfumery? And now this!"

Sally was close to tears. She needed an answer. "Am I going crazy?"

"No, dear, you're not. I've heard about this kind of thing, but never experienced it myself. I think you lived here before in a past life. Or many of them. You know too much about . . .

well, everything to have remembered this from simply one life here!" Her mother smiled at her.

"My past life? I lived before?"

"Some people think we all do," her mother said. "After we die to this life, we go to heaven, and then we get to come back. As they say, 'Life goes on.'"

"Then I'm not crazy?"

"No. The opposite in fact. Your brain is more alert than most, is all. More than mine, in fact."

Releasing a huge sigh of relief, Sally exclaimed. "Oh, I'm so glad! Now, I can enjoy my trip!"

"Yes. And all the places you loved before. Perhaps you're the reason we were compelled to not only make this trip but to bring you along with us as well," her father said.

"Compelled?"

Her father nodded. "Perhaps your guardian angel wanted you to reconnect with Paris again. Maybe you're meant to be that artist you once were, after all."

Epilogue:

That trip was over thirty years ago. Sally's parents and her friends have always encouraged her artistic talent. She has made many trips back to Paris, and in some parts of the city, her reaction is exactly the same as it was on that first trip. She finds old friends and new clues to the life she once led in Paris. Sally has also returned recently from yet another foray in Paris with her husband. She tells me that Paris has not lost one ounce of its majesty or magic for her.

Sally has not only lived up to her destiny, but she has

thrived on the knowledge that she very likely was an artist in Paris hundreds of years ago. Today she is not only a gifted painter and enjoys her canvases, paints, brushes and the inspiration that comes from heaven through her hands, but she is also successful graphic artist.

Sarasota Flyby

 was touring for my last novel, *Wings of Destiny*, in my mother's home state of Florida. It was the first leg of two weeks of intensive media, and prior to my day in Tampa, St. Petersburg and Sarasota, I had been up all night long in New York City as a participant on *The Joey Reynolds Radio Show*. This radio program is one of those live, on-air, midnight to dawn things in which the host's guests are live in the studio. I've done late-night radio shows, but usually they are from the comfort of my own home over the telephone. This, of course, translates to: Sleep immediately after the show.

Well, this show went on and on and I had to be on a train out of New Jersey at five-thirty in the morning, headed for Washington, D.C., where I was scheduled to do a live morning drive-time radio program, followed by two more taped radio programs and a television spot before catching an evening flight to Florida. I not only had to be awake and coherent, but look good as well. By the time I got on the train to Washington, D.C., I decided looking good was out of the question. I'd settle for alive.

My brain rattled more than the train wheels against the tracks. By the end of the day I was hungry and exhausted and my mental faculties at the age of fifty were definitely not what they'd been at twenty-five when my son was a newborn, surely the last time I'd been forced by God, nature and circumstances to stay awake all night long.

Only through divine grace and the forceful hand of Emily Lacie, the owner of a media escort service who took my condition seriously and plunked me into a motel room for a three-hour nap before my plane departed, was I saved from being admitted to a hospital.

With three hours of rest, I was functioning well enough to get a cab to the airport, board the plane and finally arrive in Tampa at midnight. Though I still found "the floor moving," a serious sign of sleep deprivation, I collapsed in yet another motel for a night's sleep before a five o'clock wake-up call and yet one more early-morning television interview.

By noon, I was in Sarasota for the filming of a one-hour interview with Kerry Kirschener. I had interviewed with Kerry a year and a half earlier for another book. He was gracious enough to book another, yet more extensive interview.

The first time I'd worked with Kerry, my media escort, Fred, and I drove through a tornado to make the airtime. This is no kidding! We looked up through a torrent of rain and saw a dark funnel-shaped cloud coming straight at us. Fred panicked. I screamed, and we turned off the street and parked the car away from any trees. The whirlwind turned aside, as if sensing our alarm and spun down a different street!

Fred looked at me, mouth agape, bug-eyed and said, "I guess we should carry on."

I don't know how I found my voice, but I did. "Please do

so," I replied, still watching the tornado disappear behind a section of buildings.

We found our way to the restaurant where we met with Kerry for a light supper before filming. Though he'd read my novel at the time, he wanted a more insightful interview. Kerry was fascinated with my stories about my grandparents who had lived in northwestern Florida nearly all their lives. We agreed that I would relate some of my family's history and how their lives influenced the story of *Elusive Love.*

The show went well, and two hours later it was "in the can," and I was on another airplane.

In October 2000, being back in Sarasota and seeing Kerry in his own home was a delightful reunion for me. He had decided he wanted to film outside on his beautiful lawn that swept out to the dock and down to the water. It was a "Chamber of Commerce" day with clear skies and just enough breeze to move voluminous clouds across the sky.

The cameraman was set up, and we began joking and chatting about my new book, *Wings of Destiny,* and the bizarre tale of how this story came to be (see *Angel Watch: Goosebumps, Signs, Dreams and Divine Nudges*).

Kerry then asked me to relate a story about my grandfather.

"During World War II, my grandfather, C. F. Manning, used to own a restaurant and bar. In those days, some of the pilots who flew for Jimmy Doolittle, and who were based in Pensacola, used to come to the bar and plunk away at my grandfather's piano. My grandfather loved airplanes, though he never owned one. I can remember my mother telling me about the air shows he used to take her to. She shared his love of aviation as well."

Just about the time I'd made this statement, we heard an

airplane overhead. We didn't think much of it. Kerry continued on.

"Jimmy Doolittle. Wasn't he the historic figure they based a movie on?"

"That's right," I replied. *"Thirty Seconds over Tokyo."*

Above us another airplane flew past. I was aware of the plane, but the show had to go on. I thought it odd because the two planes followed each other so closely.

"Who starred in that? Do you remember?" Kerry asked nonplussed by the interference.

"James Stewart," I replied.

I had no sooner made this statement than a group of four jets in perfect formation flew overhead. The sound of their engines was so loud that the cameraman halted us.

"Kerry, I have to take that over."

"Why?" Kerry asked.

"Audio interference," the cameraman replied.

"Okay," Kerry said looking upward. "That's weird."

Kerry shook off the eerie feeling he had, and we repeated the prior dialogue.

"That was *Thirty Seconds over Tokyo,*" I replied for the second time.

Again, the same formation of jets flew directly overhead.

"Not again!" Kerry stood up, shielded his eyes and watched the planes pass overhead.

"This is crazy," the cameraman said, walking toward us, looking skyward. "If they don't stop, I'll never get this shot."

Kerry looked at me, his blue eyes narrowed, a wry smile on his lips. "What are you, a witch?"

"I beg your pardon?"

Kerry's broad smile gave away the fact that he was teasing me. "I've lived here for sixteen years. No airplane has ever flown over this house. Not even in a bad storm. I do not live under a flight path. Military or otherwise."

"What are you saying?" I asked dumbfounded.

"Think about it, angel lady. The last time you were here, you were a near miss for some freak tornado. But you kept driving on like it was a walk in the park for you. Now you sit here telling me about your grandfather, aviation, World War II, the military and bombing raids. Do you not see a pattern here?"

I burst into laughter as my eyes shot to the sky. "Way to go, Grandpa!"

I stood up and gave Kerry a high five.

Kerry turned to the cameraman. "Did you get it?"

"The flyby?" he asked.

"Yes. How could I not?"

"Then, I want to keep it. Start rolling. Let's address this as part of the show."

We sat down, the cameraman took his place and gave us the count. Then cue.

Kerry resumed. "Folks, right here you've seen a demonstration of what Catherine is talking about in her *Angel Watch* book. Is her grandfather trying to make his presence known to her? To us? Can angels contact us on earth? Can they manipulate even flight paths? And how do they do this? You be the judge. All I can tell you is that this is a first for me."

I smiled. "How much do you want to bet it's not the last, Kerry?"

"No bets, thanks anyway." He glanced upward once again.

"Do you have any relatives, dead or alive, who ever won the lottery? Maybe they could drop a winning ticket in my mailbox!"

"Not that I know of, but if a ticket shows up, you'll have your proof, won't you?"

"I suppose you want half the winnings," he said.

"You keep it. As long as you have angels, you'll see . . . you'll always have bounty of all kinds."

christopher's Guardian portrait

arrived at the Barnes and Noble in Fort Worth after battling a rainstorm with my car. The storm won. I got lost four times trying to find my way to the bookstore on unfamiliar roads and missing my exit only to find that my directions were wrong, and the exit I was on was the correct one after all.

I was to meet my community relations representative, Christopher Cleveland, once I got to the store. While I was having Christopher paged, I wandered into the Starbucks thinking to get a snack because I hadn't eaten since early that morning, and it was past supper time now.

Christopher was a delight and not only had my signing table ready for me, he bought me a huge latte and a double-chocolate cake that was nearly sinful. I am a firm believer that when things aren't going right, get out the chocolate.

I finished my latte and cake, and Christopher then escorted me to where he'd personally seen to the setup of my table.

There on an easel was a huge painting of a guardian angel and a small child.

I stopped dead in my tracks.

"Where did this painting come from?" I asked, feeling goose bumps crawling over my shoulders. "I mean, is it for sale? Can I buy it or one like it?"

"No. It's special. It's mine."

"Yours?"

"Actually, it was my grandmother's. It's an antique. Do you like it?"

"Like it? I remember seeing one quite similar at my Grandmother Grace's house."

"No way," Christopher said.

We both stared at the painting, speechless for a moment.

"I've never shared this with anyone," Christopher said.

"That's okay. I never told anyone how I used to go into my grandmother's bedroom and look at that painting she had in a frame on her dressing table. I don't know what happened to it. Though I do have a little statue of the Blessed Virgin that was hers."

Christopher rubbed his arms.

"What's the matter?"

"Chills," he said.

I laughed. "Those aren't chills. I think that is your grandmother and my grandmother sharing a chuckle. I think they are trying to tell us they are both here watching over us."

"Just like the guardian angel in the picture?" Christopher asked.

"Something like that," I answered. "You know, it's funny, because I never particularly liked my Grandmother Grace. She was quite old when I was born, well into her seventies. So by the time I knew her, she was feeble, sick and very curt."

"Cranky, you mean," Christopher laughed.

"You can say that again. But it is strange. About twenty years ago I met a woman at a charity function in Houston who claimed she was psychic. She came up to me and said she saw my grandmother. Instantly, I assumed she meant my mother's mother. 'Ethel,' I said to her.

"'No,' the woman replied. 'She says her name is Grace. I love that name, don't you? She's holding roses for you. She loves you very much, and she said she is your guide.'"

Christopher was stunned. "She knew all that?"

"She was on target." I looked back at the painting. "I haven't heard from Grandmother Grace for a long time. I wonder why she picked today?" I mused.

"Maybe she didn't pick it. Maybe you did," Christopher said wisely.

"Maybe I've been ignoring her. Maybe she wanted her own story in my next book."

Christopher smiled. "I'd lay my money on it."

About this time several people started coming up and asking about the book, and I began the fun part of signing, getting to meet new angel watchers.

The evening ran an hour longer than anticipated. I should have been famished. I wasn't. I should have been tired. I wasn't. I came away from that magical night with at least a dozen new angel stories from people I'd met in the store.

Just as I was leaving, Christopher came by to see me off.

I shook his hand, and as I did, he said, "I will tell you what my grandmother always used to say to me."

"What was that?" I asked.

"Sleep with the angels."

I dropped my jaw. "No way."

"Don't tell me."

I nodded. "I remember Grace saying that to me one time when I spent the night at her house."

"Wow! She really did want to make a connection with you, Catherine."

"I believe she did at that."

I drove to my hotel that night promising that in the future, when I signed off on my e-mails and letters, I would abide by Grace's wish and close all my correspondence with "sleep with the angels."

So, please, you, too, remember to sleep with the angels.

Star of Hope

t approximately seven o'clock on a winter Friday morning, I was driving my three Golden Retrievers to the vet to have their weekly bath when, under one of the freeway bridges, I saw an entire homeless family.

They were huddled close to one of the concrete pilings, the two children asleep in their mother's arms. The father was standing just looking down at them.

I had stopped at the red light and couldn't help but witness their pain and loneliness. Their tragedy was so tangible that Bebe and Junior raced to the window in the back of the Tahoe to watch them.

"Let's say a prayer for them," I said aloud.

I know dogs can't pray. At least I don't think they can. Maybe they do. If so, I apologize for my ignorance on the matter.

"Please, God, send them someone to help."

At that moment, I had thought to turn my car to the shoulder, park and walk over to them. However, I was in the middle lane, the car behind me was already honking at me to get going, and I did what all "onlookers" do. I left.

I dropped the doggies off for their baths and began the drive back home. Approaching the same underpass, this time I pulled over in the far left lane so that I could drive up beside the family. The least I could do was give them some money, I thought.

I know it had not been ten minutes from the time I said my prayer to the time I returned.

When I reached the intersection, lo and behold, I saw a van with the words "Love in Action" written on the side. Underneath this was "Star of Hope." Two men were shaking hands with the mother and the father. The children, now awake, looked up with smiling faces. It was a miracle in action right before my eyes!

Everyone who lives in Houston knows of the Star of Hope Mission that has been a privately funded Christian institution since before World War I. It is our city's pride and joy. These vans and the drivers and ministers of love who man them travel the city looking for those in need.

The moment I saw the truck, I burst into tears and thanked God for the Star of Hope.

Wiping my eyes, pressing my foot to the gas pedal, I drove away saying, "Boy! That was fast!"

A Ring for Kelly

om and Kelly have been in love for many years. Because they were both establishing themselves in their new law careers they were willing to put their wedding and marriage off until they could afford their dream ceremony.

One of the pieces of this divine plan was the perfect ring for Kelly. Both Tom and Kelly wanted something unusual. Something so special, a ring so meaningful that it would bespeak their devotion every time either of them looked at it.

Whenever Kelly had a chance between dashing from her office to the courtroom and to yet another meeting, she would stop in at the jeweler's to see new styles that might have arrived. However, nothing moved her. Tom checked the catalogs from jeweler's that came in the mail, but nothing was special enough. The garbage pail was filling with old catalogs and flyers, and Kelly had given up hope she'd ever find a setting she liked.

Finally, they realized that what they both wanted was an antique ring. This gave them new hope. Surely, that magical ring was waiting out there . . . somewhere in an antique store.

Weekend jaunts to the area antique shops rendered the

same result. There was no ring for Kelly.

This past June, Tom and Kelly finally cleared their calendars long enough to take an overdue and much-needed dream vacation to France. Kelly's parents own a chalet in the French Alps where the air is crystal clean, the mountain views are spectacular, and the food and wines replenish the body's longing for the superlative.

For over a week, they rested, read, biked, hiked, lazed and enjoyed each other's company. They met new friends and reacquainted themselves with old ones. The responsibilities and hassles of city life faded away like morning fog. So, too, did their thoughts of wedding plans and their nonproductive ring hunt.

They were ecstatic just being alive and being together.

All too soon, the day came when they had to return to Paris to catch their flight back to Houston.

They arrived at Orly Airport only to discover that their particular flight had been canceled due to bad weather. There were no other flights to Houston that day. They would be forced to spend the rest of the day and that night in Paris.

Once they'd found a hotel room and checked in, Tom said to Kelly, "Just the thought of leaving all this beauty is depressing."

"I agree," Kelly said. "Too bad we can't take some of it with us."

"Then let's do!" Tom said taking her hand.

"Do what?"

"How cool would it be if I could find an antique French desk for my office?"

"Don't tell me that battered rent-a-desk hasn't grown on you yet," Kelly joked.

"This is Paris! We have the whole day. We should be able to find something . . . well, special here."

Smiling, Kelly said, "You're right. We'll have something to always remind us of these wonderful days we've had."

After checking with the concierge for a list of reputable stores, Kelly and Tom were off to the hunt.

Down main thoroughfares and winding side streets, Tom and Kelly immersed themselves in Paris. They stopped for coffee at a sidewalk café but still continued their hunt.

In a charming, out of the way store, Tom inspected yet another desk that was light years out of their price range.

"What do you think, sweetheart?" Tom asked tracing his fingers over the inlaid wood.

"Beautiful. Incredible. If you're the king of France."

"Hey, don't knock it. It belonged to the king of France," Tom laughed.

Kelly wandered to the right side of the store, mindlessly gazing at the art nouveau lamps and impressionist lithographs. She came upon a glass-enclosed jewelry case. Leaning over she smiled at pretty turn-of-the-century bracelets and necklaces.

Suddenly, her breath caught in her lungs. Her heart stopped.

Twinkling up at her was a dazzling diamond ring. If she'd fashioned the ring herself, she knew she couldn't have done a more perfect job.

"Tom . . ."

"Yeah?" Tom was crouched on the floor inspecting another desk's underside.

"I . . . I found something."

"Louis the Fourteenth or Louis the Fifteenth?"

She swallowed hard. "Kelly the First!" Excitement filled her voice.

Tom stood immediately. "What did you say?" Then he looked at her beaming face. Her smile shot to his heart.

"I . . . I think I've found my ring!"

"You can't be serious," he said and was at her side in two strides.

Tom peered into the case. "My God, that's it!"

Tom called the proprietor over, who unlocked the case. Tom slipped the ring on Kelly's finger.

"Wow. Perfect fit," Tom said with a hush.

Kelly was speechless. "It's as if it was made for me," she whispered.

Tom inquired about the price and discovered that the ring was not only a larger diamond than he'd hoped to be able to afford, the price was half of what Tom had thought to spend for Kelly's ring.

That night, with the famed Eiffel Tower as witness, Tom formally asked Kelly to be his bride. As he tells us, in a moment of "weakness" she said "YES!"

Tom and Kelly's engagement story is validation not only that their union is divinely driven, but that they have the double good luck of cost-conscious shopping angels!

Spiritual
Visitations

he visitations described by the stories in this section deal with human contact with a departed spirit, both those known to the individual and those not known.

These are not "ghost" stories meant to frighten. These are loving encounters in which souls wish to either give us warnings to help save us or our families, or information about their lives while they were incarnated on earth, usually involving an unresolved issue. These issues can be a lack of expressed love for the person still alive or in some cases, a wrong that must be made right.

Much of our fiction, television series and films deal with "spirits" or "ghosts" speaking through mediums or appearing to a psychic to solve a crime. This kind of story is becoming more common than was previously known simply because our law enforcement agencies now employ psychics and mediums as part of their investigative process. Between DNA-matching technology and trained law enforcement psychics, today's criminal isn't going to get away with much now and in the future.

The stories in this section concern visitations by deceased persons who appear to the person involved while that person is awake. These are not dreams, though the person having the encounter may be asleep when the experience begins. However, they are fully conscious and cognizant when the spirit manifests.

Manifestations are not always in full human form.

"Orb activity" is bouncing balls of light, both large and small, similar to a "Tinkerbell" effect. During the appearance of the lights, those sensitive to the spirit will either feel cold or heat; they may get "impressions" of emotions; they may hear and/or record, on a standard recorder, the voice of the departed soul/spirit.

These are not experiences from trained forensic mediums or professionals. These are real stories from ordinary people. I have been gathering these stories for years. Some date back to my childhood in Indiana.

All are unforgettable.

The Medical Team from the Other Side

Alvin, Texas. 1973.

t the age of twenty-one, my friend Vicki found she was pregnant. Though her pregnancy was normal, as the weeks rolled on she felt compelled to read the Bible. Not once or twice daily, but sometimes for the better part of the day. When she could not sleep, she read the Bible. It went with her everywhere.

Being raised Catholic, Vicki had a sound religious upbringing, but never before had she felt this urgency to "fill herself up spiritually" as she did during those months of her pregnancy with her first child.

When Andrew was born, Vicki soon realized the reason her angels were preparing her spiritually for her days ahead. Andrew was born with an absence of nerve endings in his intestines. In other words, Andrew's colon was dead. He had no bowel movements.

At first, the doctors at the hospital in Alvin, Texas, where she delivered misdiagnosed Andrew and told Vicki and her then-husband, Andy, that their baby had cystic fibrosis. In all likelihood he would die.

The doctors then hooked infant Andrew up to an IV and were feeding him charcoal through a tube in his nose. Horrified at this treatment, Vicki became enraged. "Are you trying to kill my son?" she blasted the nurses, but they brushed her off as an overwrought new mother.

Whether it was her own adrenaline rush or urging from her angels Vicki will never really know, but once the doctors and nurses had left the room, she ripped the tube out of Andrew's nose, withdrew the IV, wrapped him up and raced down the hall, clutching her son to her chest. She got to a pay phone and called her husband to come get her.

"I will not let them do this to our baby! They'll kill him if he stays here. I just know it."

"We'll find a way, Vicki," Andy said hanging up the phone and racing out the door to his car.

"I won't let you die, Andrew," she said through her tears as she left the hospital behind. "There has to be another way. There has to be."

Andy picked her up a block away, and all the way home, Vicki prayed harder than she ever had.

That same night, Vicki dreamed about a team of doctors who told her that Andrew did not have cystic fibrosis.

"You must get another opinion," they told her in the dream. "Go to the children's hospital in Houston," they told her.

The next morning, Vicki immediately telephoned Texas Children's Hospital in Houston. Within hours, Vicki had found Dr. Franklin Harberg, who took Andrew's case. Upon examination, Dr. Harberg discovered that Andrew had a rare disease known as Hirschsprung's disease.

"Vicki, there is only one cure. We must give him an ileostomy. It's a new procedure, but we're having good results with it."

"How new? And what does it entail?" she asked.

The doctor took a deep breath. "We must take out his large intestine."

"All of it?" Vicki was shocked. She'd never heard of ileostomies or even colostomies at the time.

"Most of the large intestine, yes. He will have to have a hole in his flesh in which to insert a tube through which his feces will pass."

"And this will save his life?"

"It's our only chance. Without it, Andrew will die."

"But what are his chances? Exactly. He's only a few days old."

"Not good, I'm afraid. Two out of ten that he'll make it."

"Let me ask you this. How long must we wait before you remove the ileostomy tube after the surgery? My other question is, can he return to normal?"

"Why, that's not done."

"You mean *you* haven't tried to correct the surgery yet? Or no one else in the medical community has tried it?"

"It's a very new surgery. . . . I can't guarantee . . ."

"How long?" she demanded.

"Two years."

"And what are my parameters to get him healthy enough to try this new procedure?" she asked.

"You're a very smart lady, I'll say that. If it's possible, and I'm not saying it is, Andrew would have to weigh at least twenty-one pounds at the age of two. But understand, it would be the first corrective surgery like that, that has ever been performed here."

"Being first doesn't frighten me, Dr. Harberg," she said, her dark eyes blazing with courage.

"I can see that. But Vicki, you must also understand, his diet is one-third of his cure. Frankly, we've never had a survivor in a baby this young from an ileostomy."

"You listen to me, Dr. Harberg. Andrew is going to live. He will not die. I can *will* him to live."

"Yes, I believe you can," Dr. Harberg replied.

"And what I can't will to happen, God will provide the rest. I'll pray about it. I'll get the answers."

During the long night after Andrew's operation, Vicki prayed for her answers. Falling asleep by Andrew's tiny crib, she was visited by a spiritual medical team of doctors. These spirits were dressed completely in white. Their voices were distinct and confident as they issued instructions.

"Your son must have all natural foods. Strained pears. Strained applesauce. Strained carrots and strained bananas. You must make these yourself. Also, oatmeal and mashed potatoes, but strained very fine."

One of the medical men with an exceptionally radiant face said, "Go to the farmer's market in Alvin where all the vegetables and fruits are fresh and have no pesticides. Ask the local farmers for their honey. It is important that the baby has this particular honey."

A third medical angel said, "Then take the honey to the hospital chemist. Ask him to make a formula that contains the honey and the equivalent of one baby jar of protein meat in every bottle the baby ingests."

And yet a fourth angel said, "The baby must have four bottles of this formula a day. If you do all that we say, your son will gain weight and meet the requirements for his surgery in two years."

In the days that followed, Vicki never once questioned the dream. She went about assembling everything she needed to create the special formula for Andrew. At first the nurses and hospital personnel laughed at Vicki. They scoffed at her tale of some dream team of doctors who clearly didn't know what they were talking about.

Finally, she found a dietitian who collaborated with a pediatric chemist to come up with exactly the formula the dream angels had told Vicki to blend.

Natural baby foods were not popular in those days of the early seventies, but Vicki stayed the course. She washed every fruit and carrot until it was spanking clean and then strained and pureed every food item herself to make certain the texture was thin enough for Andrew to digest.

For two years, Vicki painstakingly monitored Andrew's diet. When the corrective surgery was finally performed, it was videotaped and taken to Japan where it became a national procedure.

During that same time, Vicki wrote a "Guide for Mothers to Natural Baby Foods" to distribute to other mothers who were battling Hirschsprung's disease.

Vicki tells me that what she learned during these crises and others is:

First, you must "address the problem."
Second, you must "release the problem."
Then you wait and let the angels show you the way.

Epilogue: As of this writing, Andrew is thirty-two years old, healthy, happy, married to Paige, and they have been blessed with a very healthy baby boy.

A Cabin in the North Woods

My La Portean friends, Dick and Marti Davis, built a log cabin in the very northern part of Michigan over thirty years ago. The land is part of a National Forest and is also, some say, hallowed Indian ground. There is truly a mystical feeling about the area near Traverse City, and it is one of the most scenic stretches of terrain in the United States in my very humble opinion. To say I love it is an understatement. It's paradise.

The air is cool, crisp and clean. The river is so clear it's blinding. Fall is a golden-hued trip to fantasyland, but winter is majestic. Ancient northern pines look like willowy fashion models wearing snowy ermine coats. The Davis's cabin, fastened like a jeweled pin in a lapel's curve, sits at the end of a forested lane. Snowbanks hug the road and the base of the structure. Even at first sight, one knows this is the house that love built.

Dick and Marti began construction on the cabin just after graduating from college. The original structure they built with their own hands, summer after summer, year after year. Today, a second floor exists that peaks into the A-framed beamed roof.

It was in the second floor bedroom with its high peaked ceiling where I slept during my visit that first winter there.

Though it was January, Christmas decorations still hung across the streets and in café windows. Twinkling lights were reflected in the diamondlike new-fallen snow. Nights brought a mystical, celestial quality to the area, which I chalked up to my leftover Christmas spirit.

During the day we browsed the shops in Traverse City, shared cappuccinos and even found some copies of my novels in the local bookstore. That night we built a grand wood fire in the fireplace while preparing dinner. Dick Davis has one of the most acute and intelligent senses of humor I've ever known. His humor ranks right up there with my father's, which I've missed constantly since his passing.

There was plenty of laughter in the house that night as we opened fine red wine to accompany the prime rib roast in the oven. Though the day had been uplifting and the night fun-filled, I still had not realized the extent of the magical influence the land itself had upon my psyche.

As I prepared for bed, I looked out over the moon-splattered snow and felt an extraordinary sense of peace flutter over me. This was a time in my life where little about my life pleased me. I missed my son incredibly. He was away at college, engaged to Christy, finding his own life. My father was deceased, and I missed him so much I ached inside. Though I was writing, I had no publisher. I worked days for my sister for her business, but it was not mine. I was more than floundering. I was adrift.

Life had become an ocean of meaningless fear. I feared everything and feared nothing, if that makes any sense. I didn't care if I lived. I didn't care if I died. I just flat didn't care. And for me, this had never happened. I have always been one who had so many things to do in a day, so many life goals, so many people to see, so many places to go, that my lists had to be outlined!

I had no direction. I had no discernable parameters of my divine path.

Looking out on that snow as I had so many times in my childhood living in Indiana, I prayed. I asked God to give me direction. Not answers. Not a million dollars.

"Just show me the way, God."

I no more than said the words when goose bumps scooted down my spine. I felt as if a pair of hands placed themselves on my shoulders. Reassuring and loving, I did not feel they were my father's hands. Nor did I think they were the hands of an angel. I don't know what I thought they were, just a pressure, really.

Still, they didn't give me direction.

I went to bed.

That night I received probably one of the most extraordinary dreams of my lifetime. Dreams of this divine nature are different from "thought-processing" dreams or dreams in which we shake out our mental woes and everyday trials. These dreams are crystal clear. You cannot only see it, but smell the air, feel or touch the individuals. Hearing is acute during these dreams. If there's music, you can remember it. There is a quality about such dreams that makes you feel as if you've stepped into another world, another dimension. It's the Twilight Zone for certain!

To this day, this dream is so real to me that I am not really positive if I dreamed it or if I was awake during it. The closest to this dream that I've come was when my grandmother appeared to me a week after her death. But I did, indeed, wake up from the first part of that dream.

This one, I'm not sure.

I heard a voice, Mr. Voice, actually, call my name. "Cathy. Wake up!"

After that initial call, I must state that I no longer heard his voice speak to me.

I sat up straight in bed and looked at the end of the bed. Standing in front of me were three men.

On the left was Cary Grant dressed in a tuxedo. He was smiling at me, holding an Oscar. He was so real; I could smell some kind of piney aftershave on him. He was a young Cary Grant, not the way he was in later years. His hair was very dark and slicked back with a lot of greasy stuff that made it shine like patent leather. I remember thinking, "Don't touch that hair. It will stain your clothes."

The second man was King Midas. He looked like a comic book King Midas at first, until he moved. Then he looked like a real man. He wasn't as tall as Cary Grant, his robes were scarlet and gold, and nearly Greek-looking rather than Middle Ages in era. There was a thick gold crown on his head; he had rather long, light brown hair, a beard and a mustache. His eyes were honey brown. He had a nice smile, but it looked like he had false teeth they were so straight across, making his mouth look boxy, which may explain why he seemed like a comic book character to me. In his hands he held a gold box filled to overflowing with huge gold coins. The coins were just spilling out of the box as if there was an abundant supply of riches available.

The third man was a magician. He wore purple or indigo blue robes and clothing. The velvet was decorated in silver and gold threads. He wore a tall pointed hat like Mickey Mouse in *Fantasia* with moons and stars on it. Then I realized that his robes held all the galaxies, and I was really looking into the universe, with stars comets whizzing by and spinning worlds in his cloak. He had very long white hair and a long silvery beard. His eyes were sky blue, and his smile was pink. His cheeks were pink as if he were a thinner, celestial Santa Claus.

In his hands was a white glowing ball. It radiated silver light, and he moved his hands around the orb, not holding it next to his flesh but rather as if he were keeping it suspended in his hands.

I wanted him to be Merlin, the magician, but he was not. He was someone else, or he represented something else.

"Who are you?" I asked.

Cary Grant said, "You remember me, don't you?"

"Yes."

Then I moved to the next man and asked the same question. "Who are you?"

"I am King Midas. I bring you wealth."

The third man said, "I am Wisdom."

They were all smiling at me benevolently. "Am I supposed to choose?"

"You may if you want," Wisdom said.

I viewed them again, left to right. "I would give up fame and fortune to have wisdom. I choose you," I said to the last man in purple with the Mickey Mouse hat.

He did not say I chose wisely, and my human ego would

have liked to know if I'd passed the test. Got the A. Made the grade.

"Watch what I do."

He then moved his hands around the ball. Placing his hand on the top and bottom of the light orb, he said, "The sun and moon."

Then he moved his hands to the right and left side.

"The earth and the stars."

Then he repeated it over and over and over. "The sun and the moon. The earth and the stars." All the while constantly moving his hands around the ball.

I was flabbergasted. And severely disappointed. "That's it?"

"The sun and the moon and the earth and the stars."

He repeated himself gazing at me with profound knowing and enlightenment in his eyes.

I have no idea if this vision was giving me the keys to life itself or if that Mickey Mouse/*Fantasia* hat had made him bonkers. I still don't know what it means.

Here I was looking for direction to my divine path, expecting an angel, and I got three guys who, though very, very real, were spewing some mumbo jumbo that wasn't helping me in the least.

What was I supposed to do with sun, moon, earth and stars? I was too old to become an astronaut. Maybe I was supposed to bone up on my Carl Sagan books. Reread Genesis? What?

At that moment, Cary Grant took a step forward. "Cathy."

"What?" I asked, near to tears.

He stretched out his arms and handed me the Oscar. I remember that the sleeves of his jacket rode up, and I could hear the scratch of wool against his white cotton tuxedo shirt.

Maybe it was silk, but it made a distinct noise.

My heart leaped and then raced as he placed the Oscar into my hands. I touched the gold, felt the metal and actually touched the edge of his fingers.

My flesh touched his flesh, and he was alive!

I felt the adrenaline race through my body like never before. My mouth went dry. My eyes flooded with tears.

"I don't understand."

"You forgot to pick this up last time," Cary said in the most distinct enunciation possible.

"Last time?"

He smiled that Cary Grant smile and nodded. "Yes."

I was still holding that Oscar, my heart exploding as all three men simply vanished.

Still feeling metal in my hands, the Oscar faded. The room went black.

The next thing I knew it was morning.

However, when I woke I was sitting bolt upright.

"Last time?" I said the words to myself as I opened my eyes.

Goose bumps riddled my body like ice water pellets.

In the past forty years I've had several unforgettable past-life dreams. Some have been recurring. All have been profound.

In several of these dreams I have known that I was a screen-play writer in Hollywood in the twenties and thirties. I believe, but don't know for absolute certainty—whoever will until we actually die—that I died in 1943. However, this profession of this truth was different.

I felt that those on the Other Side gave this vision to me.

I did not, nor do I now believe this was simply an extension of my consciousness, though I do not rule out that possibility. Obviously, if my mind is the repository of all my past-life information, my mind could make this vision. If so, then my mind created people in the flesh, one of whom I actually touched.

After profound reflection over many years on this experience and before committing it to paper for others to read, I believe this was a true visitation from beings/spirits from the Other Side.

I had prayed that night for God to show me the way.

Ever since my experience with *Romancing the Stone* and *The Jewel of the Nile,* when I had the chance to go on the 20th Century Fox Studio lot, visit the actors, the crew, the sound stages and offices of Michael Douglas, I have believed that my reconnection from that former life to Hollywood and/or films had been made.

This experience took place ten years after *Romancing the Stone.* For those ten years I had made several stillborn stabs at a screenwriting career, but my feet were still very cold.

In a word, I was chicken.

To throw my work into the shark-infested waters of film-dom was a fate worse than death to me. Writing was one thing, but I knew so little about screenplays. I'd rationalized my lack of courage to myself by convincing myself that screenplay writing was a completely different brain function, and one I did not possess. I was a novelist. Wasn't that enough for God?

Apparently not.

That's what these men of vision were saying to me.

They were saying you want to know what you came to earth to do? This is it. Now do it!

At this point in my life, this was the second time I'd been told what to do by "beings" from the Other Side. The first time was when my dying father told me I was to chronicle spiritual/angelic stories, such as I'm doing with this book.

I was chicken about these stories as well. I still am. I'm not certain if this is courage I am displaying or fear of retribution when I finally do get to the Other Side, so that when I am asked if I performed my "destiny tasks" I can say (with knocking knees) "yes."

It has been ten years since I witnessed the three visions in the north woods. Two and a half years ago, I put my novel writing days aside, temporarily, and jumped into the unknown.

For many years I had taken classes and dabbled in screenwriting, trying to learn all I could. I watched movies, wrote some horrible screenplays and gleefully shredded them in my shredder. Even when I wanted to give up, the angels would not let me. Their visitations in my dreams, and giving me "signs" along the way, have helped me to keep my focus.

As of this writing, I have now completed nine screenplays and formed my own film production company. I now am represented by a film management company based in Los Angeles and New York. In addition, a Hollywood film agent has agreed to represent my work and my husband, Jed Nolan's, work as an independent film producer. We have more than fifteen projects that are constantly being pitched as television movies of the week, Hallmark Hall of Fame features for television and a "reality" television series based on this book about angels and my previous book, *Angel Watch.* Several of my feature film scripts are being shopped to large production companies and major studios. We have formed alliances with two production companies, and by the time this book is published we should have finalized a coproduction deal for five of my scripts with a third company, God willing. Though this process of moving my words from paper to film could still take years, I know I must "hang in there."

I have done something that, for me, has heretofore been unfathomable. To leave the safety net of my novel writing career on that simmering back burner, leave Texas and my son and granddaughter and move to California, has been a true test of "facing one's fears." Jed and I have written a business plan for our company, which was the most difficult writing I have ever had to execute. I have always been a hard worker, but in addition to long hours and no time off for fun, I have learned more in the past three years than I have in the past twenty. I have met with fund-raisers, investment counselors, investors, producers, studio heads, development executives, lawyers and accountants, and by some miracle I have actually been able to understand a great deal of what has been explained to me. I am learning a new business from the cement floor up!

I have put my faith in my angel's words. My soul tells me that in addition to my books, I must pursue this path to making films. I don't pretend to be a filmmaker, because I am not. I am a storyteller, and it is the story that is the genesis for film.

I have no idea if any of my projects will ever be made into film or not, but I do know one thing.

Believing is one thing.

Believing with action is divine.

On Cat's Paws

June 20, 2001.

uring the late night of June 19, 2001, from one in the morning until nearly dawn, I was the guest on the Art Bell show, *Coast to Coast.* Even though Mr. Bell was off on an early vacation, my experience with Ian Punnett was something I will never forget. I did the radio program from my own home, and just being on the telephone that long was a new experience for me. The audience was not only intelligent and willing to share their own angel "sightings," they were more awake than I!

By the next morning I was just plain worn out. However, I was scheduled to be in Dallas, a five-hour trip to the north, for a book signing at the Barnes & Noble there.

I was determined to catch at least a few hours sleep before hitting the road at nine that morning.

It was still dark when I settled into my bed. I had just turned off the lights when I heard the jingling tags on my Golden Retriever, Bebe, as she came up the stairs.

"Bebe? Is that you?" I asked.

Bebe has this funny grunt she gives when I talk to her. She

sounds more like a pig than a dog. Though it doesn't sound ladylike at all, other Golden owners have told me that their females make this sound as well. So, I am fairly certain she's not really a pig, nor does she have pig tendencies.

"Lay down next to the bed, Bebe," I said. "I have to sleep."

I reached down to touch Bebe, but was so exhausted I didn't bother to reach that far. If I had, I would have fallen out of the bed and would never have had the energy to climb back up.

"Okay, girl. You stay there."

I no more than said these words, when I felt Bebe jump onto the bed with me.

Bebe may sound like a pig, but the worst part is that she is as fat as a pig. In fact, she looks like a sheep. Pretty, but a sheep.

Okay, it's my fault. I give her everything she shouldn't have. Iced sugar cookies. Crackers. Taco chips. Ice cream. She loves 'em. What can I say? I spoil her just as much as Beau and Junior. The boys, of course, have a higher metabolism. They look good. They're guys. Girls? Well, it takes more maintenance. She needs a doggie workout room. Doggie treadmill. You get the picture.

So, when my seventy-five-pound Bebe jumps on the bed, you pretty much know someone is there.

After who I thought was Bebe jumped onto the bed, I started to roll over and pet her.

The hairs on the back of my neck stood on end. Chills sailed down my arms.

"You're not Bebe," I whispered to myself.

The room was pitch-black. The air seemed to hang stagnant under the whirling ceiling fan. Time stood still.

I could feel the impression of four legs on the bed. This ghost was an animal, all right. It certainly wasn't human.

Several years ago, I established some "spiritual" rules in my life after so many interrupted nights. One of them was that no ghost or spirit was allowed in the bedroom. No peeking over my shoulder. No scaring me in the middle of the night. No talking. No passing notes.

I need my sleep. Everybody does.

This particular night, I did not feel anything malevolent or harmful. Nor did I feel anything peaceful. I was simply aware of this presence.

"Why, this is a cat!" I suddenly realized.

I peered through the darkness to the floor below me. "Bebe?"

Snort. Bebe gave her pig-grunt . . . from the floor. Not on the bed!

The idea or notion came to me that the following day I was going to meet someone whose cat had just died.

"Okay, you've made your point," I said to the cat spirit. "You can leave now."

With those words, the little kitty ghost vanished as did the feel of the weight of its paws on the bed beside me.

I once heard from a Hindu, actually, that the most powerful prayer on earth was the Lord's Prayer. I say it every night before I go to bed. Wrapped in the protection of that prayer, I was asleep in thirty seconds.

The trip to Dallas was great until I entered Dallas proper. The sky had filled with horrific thunderclouds and a terrible storm moved over the city. The traffic was jammed due to construction that seemed purposefully aimed at making me late for my signings. Rain pelted the car, hail skittered across the exit ramps, lighting flashed, thunder boomed and tornados touched down.

I got lost four times but I finally made it.

While signing books at the Barnes & Noble, a very pretty young woman came up to me and asked for a copy of my book. I signed it for her, and she asked if she could share an angel story with me.

I was amazed at her story and agreed I would put it in my book.

We chatted a bit longer, and she was about to leave when she said, "I don't know why I was compelled to come over here. I didn't even know you would be here. But I was wanting a book on angels tonight."

"Why tonight?" I asked. "Do you need them especially now?"

"It's not that really. I suppose this will sound silly to a stranger, but I had to put my cat to sleep last week and I was just missing her so much."

"A cat?" I asked.

Those old goose bumps bumped around on my arms like Mexican jumping beans.

"Yeah. She was so sweet."

As she spoke I remembered my experience the night/morning before with the cat ghost. "She was kinda heavy, right? Like about twenty pounds?"

"Eighteen."

In my mind's eye I could see a long-tailed cat, gray and black or black with gray markings. "I had a cat once but it was a Manx. It didn't have a tail," I said.

"Oh, no. She had a tail. A long pretty tail."

"And she was gray or black and . . ."

"Yes! She was black with white and gray markings."

My eyes were as wide as full moons. I think even to this day I'm more amazed at the things that happen to me than anyone else. Perhaps it's true that the more one is open to such "happenings," the more you see; not that these things weren't always going on, because they were. It is simply that these days I'm not so quick to think it is "just my imagination."

"How did you know?" the woman asked.

I told her about my night visitor and that I'd had the impression I would meet someone whose cat had recently passed away.

"Then she's alive . . . I mean on the Other Side," she said happily.

"Yes."

"You have no idea what this means to me! I thought I was going crazy, because three times this week, I thought I'd felt her jump into bed with me. She died in my arms, you see, while I was sitting in bed with her. She'd been so sick, and she had always loved being in that nice soft bed."

"I'd say she was still partial to the bed, dear."

We chuckled a bit longer.

I continued. "I find this all very interesting because many people have asked me if pets have souls. I have always believed that they did, but have never seen one. I've heard of people having near-death experiences and seeing their departed pets when they die and then come back. I have even seen photographs from photographers who specialize in 'ghostly' photos in which dogs, cats and horses appear. It would only make sense to me that anyone or any pet whom you love and who loves you back, even if in the form of loyalty, would live on. Energy is energy. It doesn't go away," I said.

"I agree. I've never seen my cat's spirit, but I have this feeling that she's there or here, with me. I loved her so much."

"I think she came to me so that I could reassure you that she knows you love her and miss her."

"Funny, isn't it?" she asked.

"What is?"

"I wasn't planning to come here tonight. Then the storm came up. And I thought to myself, maybe I can find an angel book. Then here you are with *Angel Watch*, and you, a stranger, had this mysterious visitation last night. So, do you think it was my cat who 'told' me to come here tonight? Or my angels?"

"Both, probably."

"Yeah, that's a lot of work when you think about it," the woman said.

"Sure is. But you know, they must think we're worth it."

Smiling, we shared a look of inner knowing that usually only occurs when long lost friends meet.

In many ways, that's what this life is all about. Meeting long lost souls we met and knew in heaven. It wouldn't surprise me a bit if we'd planned this entire new meeting on the Other Side, in the hope of helping each other.

Maybe we don't give ourselves enough credit for the little things we do for each other. Wouldn't it be ironic if we were the angels?

Hometown Halloween

think it is important to understand that my hometown of La Porte, Indiana is located only twenty-some-odd miles from the birthplace of Frank L. Baum, the creative genius behind *The Wizard of Oz* series of books. It is impossible not to think of scarecrows, tin men, little people and magical homecomings when October moves into northwestern Indiana. Maple trees turn to gold and flame, and the profusion of hardwoods ringing every one of our seven lakes reflect glowing amber light that, when you scrunch your eyes half closed, looks like a yellow brick road to heaven.

All my life, I've said that La Porte has been mysteriously encapsulated in some time warp that never moved much past my birth date of 1947. Many are the friends I've brought from large cities and even other small towns to my hometown, and no one can believe it. La Porte is like Sleepy Hollow and Capra's Bedford Falls from *It's a Wonderful Life,* all rolled into one.

In the center of town stands the steeple-topped, red stone county courthouse with its precision moving clock tower looking down on the residents. Though the current structure was built in 1893, it was erected on the site of the original courthouse constructed in 1835 with its replacement built in 1849. It was in those very halls and chambers where, on more than one occasion, my father fought as a young attorney for justice, first as a prosecuting attorney and later as a civil attorney. At the end of his life he was the county attorney.

La Porte still has a Fourth of July parade, Lion's Club Pancake Breakfasts and a county fair where my niece and nephews enter their handiwork and baking in 4-H exhibits just as I did when I was their age. It is the kind of Americana most people believe exists only in the past, but in reality is very much with us today.

Radiating from the center of the courthouse, located just two blocks from the railroad station, are two main thoroughfares, Michigan and Indiana avenues, which are lined shoulder to shoulder with magnificent maple trees planted over a hundred years ago. When I was in grade school, the Boy Scouts used to tap the trees for the maple sap for the maple syrup they sold for various charities about town. I can remember that sweet maple aroma emanating from huge black cauldrons stirred by some of my school friends and their parents. What fun it was to buy that syrup sold by the Maple City Cadets and Boy Scouts.

Architectural dowagers of the Victorian era grace the "avenues," each distinct in their structure, no two alike and each whispering echoes of lives past, yet sustaining the families that live inside them. Though all holidays are celebrated in La Porte, it's during Halloween when these antique homes flood the city with an ambiance found only in long-ago America.

Carved pumpkins and basketball-sized chrysanthemums

climb stone steps to balustraded front porches. Autumn grapevine wreaths decorated with gourds, pinecones, Indian corn and fall flowers hang on leaded glass doors. Garlands of fall leaves, raffia and cornhusks drape entrances and embrace gas lampposts and mailboxes. Teepees of cornstalks on front lawns remind onlookers that this was once Indian ground, sacred and blessed.

When the sun sets across the farmland and cool evening mist rises against orange-blasted clouds, the air currents drift like gypsy fairies over fallen bronze autumn leaves, lifting them into tiny whirlpools of color. The leaves scamper according to the mysterious invisible puppeteer fingers that move them, until they come to rest a block away.

This portrait exists as much today as it did back in the 1950s when I was a child. On Halloween night all the kids in our neighborhood went trick-or-treating. We went to Mrs. Parker's house where she baked iced sugar cookies in the shapes of pumpkins, each with our own name on it. The only bad part about this wonderful treat was that Mrs. Parker only made *one* cookie for each kid. It was also a clever way for her to know who the intruders into the neighborhood were and who belonged. Then we went to Mrs. Dompky's house for cider and doughnuts. Popcorn balls were my favorite at Mrs. Mellenthin's house, and Mother made pumpkin chiffon tarts for all our friends.

It wasn't until I was in high school that the treats changed to Hershey bars and bubble gum. Still, the best part of Halloween was when we kids would gather and compare our treasures. This was the time when we would tell daring stories of adventure and near misses with "intruders," kids from other neighborhoods. The boys would tell how they outran bullies or high school "big" guys. The girls would extol their terror when one of the boys jumped out of the hedges with blood-curdling screams. From these stories we would then move on to the most horrifying of all . . . our ghost stories.

It was in 1958 on Halloween night when my father came home from a meeting, or so we'd been told. That night it was Daddy's turn to tell the best ghost story we had ever heard.

My parents' good friends, Bob and Gerri Zimmermann, lived with their five children in a very old house off 18th Street in La Porte. The house was an enormous frame structure with high ceilings, elaborate crown molding and heavy oak interior doors. A wide wooden staircase wound gracefully to the sec-ond story. When the Zimmermanns moved into the house strange things began happening. At night, when Gina or Kathy would turn out the lights, the lamp would automatically go back on. Month after month, such electrical phenomenon con-tinued to occur, enough so that Bob called in an electrician to investigate.

Because the house was old, it only stood to reason that per-haps faulty wiring was to blame. However, after replacing out-dated electrical wiring at quite some expense, the oddity of lamps turning themselves off and on continued.

It wasn't long before one of the children posed the notion that the house was haunted.

Bob didn't believe in ghosts. What was dead was dead, he declared to the children.

A few months after the electrician left, the entire family was downstairs putting a puzzle together when they heard an upstairs bedroom door close.

"The wind must have blown the door closed," Bob said rising. "I'll check the windows."

"It's cold out," Gerri said. "All the windows are shut."

"That's ridiculous. How could the door shut if the wind didn't do it?"

"It's the ghost, Daddy," the children said in unison.

Bob went upstairs to check on the windows. Just as Gerri had said, the windows were all shut and locked.

Month after month, a new prank was being played on the Zimmermann family by their ghostly intruder.

Finally, Bob decided he wanted a formal investigation into the matter. He called my father, the local sheriff and two deputies as witnesses.

The group gathered at the house and stood in the foyer where the staircase rises to the second floor.

The sheriff was skeptical. The witnesses were totally disbelieving. My father said he "reserved judgment."

Bob asked the ghost to show himself or herself by turning on a lamp, closing a door or moving an object. Everyone waited. Nothing happened.

For over an hour, Bob continued to command the ghost to show itself. Silence.

Finally, the sheriff, wanting to get home to his dinner, frustratingly took off his belt and asked for several other belts from the men present. He linked them together between the two newel posts of the staircase.

"I defy any spirit in this house to take that belt off this staircase!" he blasted.

In less than ten seconds, the buckle lifted, the straight metal piece moved by itself out of the round hole in the leather, the strap unfurled and the belts fell straight to the floor.

All witnesses stared in shock and disbelief.

"You see?" Bob said. "My house is haunted."

Everyone moved out of the house with lightening speed.

This eyewitness event was the "meeting" my father had been to.

When he told the story to all of us sitting Indian-style in a circle, we were saucer-eyed and shivering with chills.

"What is very interesting," Daddy said, "was that I didn't feel like any harm would come to us. I don't think the ghost is a bad fellow."

We gasped. "All ghosts want to scare us!"

"I'm not so sure about that," Daddy said. "Maybe they just want us to know they exist. Maybe what we should be doing is praying for them instead of being afraid of them."

Daddy smiled. "Helping our loved ones who have left the earth is what Halloween is all about. It's more than candy and cookies. Tomorrow is All Saint's Day. In ancient times the early Christians wanted to make the earth the most blessed place imaginable, so they burned bonfires all night to cleanse the air of evil thoughts and deeds to make way for the ones who were the most loving and courageous of people. The saints were good people, helping others and giving their lives for goodness. So, you see, Halloween is really a night of prayer. Much like Christmas Eve. We can help that sad ghost over at the Zimmermann house by praying that he or she finds their way to heaven."

My father left us with our thoughts.

I can remember looking down at my horde of candy thinking it didn't quite seem so special anymore. I had been going around taking treats, when maybe I should have been giving something to someone instead. I wasn't very proud of myself right then.

That night as Nancy and I laid in our twin beds staring up at the ceiling and talking as we always did, we said some prayers together.

"I hope that ghost leaves the Zimmermann house," Nancy said.

"Me, too. I bet he's really sad. If you're dead, shouldn't you be happy?"

"I dunno. I was just thinking, I can't go visit Laura until her ghost is gone because I'd be too scared."

"That, too," I laughed thinking once again, Nancy had such a gift for nailing the practical and obvious.

Years later the Zimmermanns sold their house and the large piece of land beneath it to a medical group who erected a huge family clinic on the premises. To this day, there are stories of lights that go off and on during the night and the elevator that mysteriously rides up to the second floor and back down when no one is in the building.

Perhaps on this coming All Hallow's Eve you who have read this story might say a little prayer that the lost soul who inhabits that "space" where the old Zimmermann house stood, will turn around, open its heart to the Light of God, see its own family on the Other Side waiting to embrace it and move on with its spiritual enlightenment.

Angela's Angelic Push

AUTHOR'S NOTE: *My friend Vicki tells this story about her daughter Angela's encounter with a spirit who saved her life in a most dramatic manner.*

ngela was in high school when she heard stories about three unusual graves by the railroad tracks. The rails ran along Interstate 10 going east to west in Houston. One of the provisions when the lines were laid was that the rail company did not disturb the three graves or the headstones of one priest and two nuns who had been buried there for years.

Angela's friends, Karen and Shea, had heard ghost stories about unusual incidents near these graves. Some of their friends had told of ghostly appearances at night and even voices. Like all ghost stories, the tales grew in proportion to the number of times told. When Shea and Karen urged Angela to go with them one night to the tracks to see the headstones, Angela was driven by curiosity to agree.

The three headstones were situated at the top of an embankment right smack-dab next to the railroad tracks. The girls parked their car, climbed up the hill and found the markers.

Straddling the tracks, Angela leaned over, using her flashlight to read the faded and eroded inscriptions on the headstones. Because it was a weekend night, there was a great deal of traffic on the interstate located not fifty yards away.

"Can you read it, Angie?" Shea asked.

Not looking up, Angela replied, "No. The light isn't good. I'm trying to make out what year they died."

"Maybe we should come back in the daytime," Karen replied, a shiver going down her spine.

Angie brushed away some dirt, hoping to find a date, but the impressions were so faint that in the dim light, it was impossible to read even the name, much less the dates of birth or death.

Angela was so intent on discovering the dates that she didn't hear Shea when she said, "Angie, come on!"

The noise of the rush of traffic, the fast moving semitrucks and a blaring ambulance filled the night. Angie kept working away at the headstone. She still did not look up.

Now Karen was screaming at Angela. "Angie! Get out of the way!"

Angela heard nothing.

Suddenly, Angie felt a hand on her shoulder. With a distinct hard shove, she was pushed right down the embankment. She rolled and tumbled to a halt.

In that split second, she looked up and saw a train come barreling down the tracks where only a millisecond before, she had been standing.

In the blink of another eye, the train was gone and Angela saw Karen and Shea standing on the other side of the tracks, shaking, crying, screaming and knowing that

Angela had surely been killed by the oncoming train.

They screamed her name.

"What?" Angela shouted back from the bottom of the embankment on the other side.

The girls rushed up to the tracks and stared down at Angela still on her backside.

"You're alive!" The shocked girls shouted happily.

"I'm alive," Angie said rising and brushing off her jeans.

"I kept yelling at you, Angie, but you didn't hear me. The traffic noise blended with the noise of the train," Shea said.

Karen hugged Angela. "Guess you didn't hear the train."

"No, I never did," Angela replied.

"What? Then how . . . ?"

"I was pushed. I felt this hand on my shoulder. If it wasn't you . . ." Angela looked at Karen who shook her head.

"It wasn't me," Karen said. "How could it be? We were on the other side of the tracks down the hill."

All three girls looked at the headstones of the priest and two nuns. Realization of their miracle filled their eyes as they looked at each other.

"Do you think it is possible?" Shea asked

Angela nodded. "Not only possible, but it happened. I don't know which one of them saved my life; maybe it was all three. But I do know it was a ghost."

Angela slowly walked over to the headstones and reverently touched all three. "Thank you for saving my life. I'll never forget you for this. Never."

The girls walked away from the train tracks that night arm in arm. When they'd planned their ghostly expedition, each had been looking for validation that spirits coexist with humans. They'd hoped to hear a voice or see a rising mist; something like they'd seen in the movies. None of them ever dreamed they would come away with an experience that would alter their perception of life and death forever.

Babies Talk

n spring 2001, my first book on angels, *Angel Watch,* had received a fair amount of attention in my then-hometown of Houston, Texas. I was fortunate to have booked several open forum discussions at local bookstores. At one particular book signing at Barnes & Noble during the questions and answers, I had related that at the age of twenty-eight, I had lost a son at birth. After the signing, one of the women in the audience asked me if I would agree to come to her church's bereavement group of parents who had lost children. Because of my personal experience, she felt that I would bond with the group. I explained that I had never spoken to such a specific and traumatized group before, and I didn't believe that I was qualified to handle the emotions of the parents. She informed me that she was a counselor and that all she expected of me was a short ten-minute talk about my book, about angels and my father's near-death experience, and hopefully these stories would give these parents encouragement and hope.

She said that there were seven couples, one single mother and one single father. Finally, I agreed to the meeting the next week.

I should mention this was a long-established Houstonian Presbyterian Christian church. This was not a "New Age" or splinter group/sect/cult. This was as traditionalist-minded, middle Americana as one could hope to find. These were ordinary people besieged by the extraordinarily tragic loss of a child. They needed more than hope; they needed to *understand.*

As the meeting started, the counselor decided not to have me speak about *Angel Watch,* but rather have each couple introduce themselves to me and give a very short scenario of who they were and how they lost their child.

This all seemed reasonable to me, and I figured the entire process would take fifteen minutes or so.

The first couple introduced themselves and began to tell me their story about how their two-year-old son died of a heart malfunction. I listened to their tearful story of how much they missed their child. It had been three years since their son's death, and to them his tragic, sudden passing was as close to them as yesterday. They were both in tears and hugged each other for comfort.

My own heart broke for them; their pain was so tangible. Sorrow flooded me as if I had lost my son all over again. I remember thinking to myself that the counselor need not have worried about there being a bond between these couples and me. In less than minutes, I was completely immersed in their grief.

As I had stated to the counselor, I had never worked with a bereavement group of any kind. In college I had a minor in psychology, but none of those classes prepared me for this. Diplomatically or psychologically, I had no idea what to say.

They only glanced at me briefly as if looking for an answer and then realized that no one could really help them. It was that hopelessness in them that triggered the following truly extraordinary and angelic experience.

I asked them, "What month of the year was your son born?"

"July," the woman answered.

"And what month did he die?"

"December."

"So, he came in on water and left on fire. He advanced."

They looked at me dumbfounded. I shook my head, wondering where on earth I had come up with those words! They didn't mean anything to me. The month of birth, I understood astrologically, because some people believe that your birth month helps to determine some of your proclivities and personality traits. Why would the month of death be important? And why was I asking it?

At that very second, I realized that I was not doing the talking here. The angels were.

I didn't argue with my Divine Source.

I surrendered, gave in and let that divine goodness deliver whatever messages it wanted to gift these grieving individuals with.

Then I asked the parents, "Is there anything in particular about your son that you want to share?"

"No."

We moved on to the next couple. They told me their names and before they even mentioned their child's name, something very strange and miraculous happened. I thought I saw a two-year-old boy standing next to the first couple. He wore a wide navy and red striped Rugby shirt. He carried a cuddly, stuffed toy bunny.

I interrupted the second couple and went back to the first couple. "Did your son have a favorite stuffed animal? A bunny in particular?" I asked.

"Why, yes," the woman replied.

"How do you know that?" the father asked.

Not being all that well versed in "seeing" departed children, I said, "It's just an impression, really." Then I asked, "Did he have a navy and red striped shirt with matching navy shorts?"

"That's the outfit we buried him in," the mother said.

"Your impressions are pretty specific," the father said.

I looked at him. "I believe your son is always with you. He has an incredible loving energy. He has not left you at all."

They appeared comforted by this information, but already there were whispers around the room, and I felt I could nearly touch the skepticism, it was so tangible. Frankly, I didn't blame any of them for not believing what they were hearing. I was saying it, and I could hardly believe it myself! I figured it was a onetime angelic connection. It couldn't happen again.

We moved on to the next set of parents. This couple's child was only six months old when she died. They told me her name, and this time within seconds, I saw a blond little girl with blue eyes standing by her mother.

Instantly, I knew the dead girl's birth month was April without asking. Because their baby was only six months old when she died, I realized that the little girl had aged on the Other Side. This was the same number of years she would have been if she had lived on this side of the Veil. The parents had *not* described their daughter to me. I asked them if she was blond and blue-eyed.

"Yes," the mother replied. Then she peered at me. "You can see her."

"She is very real to me. She wants me to tell you that she came into your life for this moment to occur. Both of you have not believed in life after death, though your hearts have been struggling to be felt. This dichotomy has caused trouble in your marriage and disrupted your personal health. She is here to save you both by showing you through me and the miracles you will experience in the future, that there is, indeed, life after death."

When I finished, the couple was in tears thanking me. I explained what I believed and felt. "My presence here is incidental to what is occurring. Your daughter would have found a conduit sooner or later. She has been aching to come through."

We moved on to the next set of parents. Their son had been only two years old when he died in an automobile accident, but the spirit who was appearing to me was a strapping sixteen-year-old, who looked hale, hearty and nearly alive. Of all the spirits that came through that night, this boy was so nearly in the flesh it was almost, but not really, frightening. When souls come through with so much love for us, there is nothing frightening about it.

This boy was very anxious to talk to his parents and me. He told me that his parents were considering divorce and that the father blamed the mother for the accident. He explained that his mother had nothing to do with his fate and that all these things had been decided by their three souls on the Other Side, prior to their incarnation on earth. He loved his parents dearly and did not want them to divorce. He wanted them to know that he was always with them, and they were never alone.

This process of each couple contacting their departed child continued for over two hours. I had intended to speak for ten minutes that night and leave. Nothing in my past experience had prepared me for the astounding occurrences that night.

The third to the last couple was quite unique. They were a beautiful couple, in their late forties, very well dressed, both with fit bodies and the kind of tans that come from leisure-time sports and activities. The husband sat with his back to his wife, his legs crossed and his arms crossed over his chest. He was clearly enduring the pain of this farce.

When I got to them, I saw their twenty-one-year-old daughter standing behind them. She had angel's wings.

The woman told me her name. I asked the man his name.

"This is absolute bullshit! How can you lead these people on like this?"

I did not reply, but looked at their daughter's spirit to reply.

"I see your daughter in Italy. She's painting. She is surrounded by angels. In a past life she was an apprentice to Raphael. She adored Michelangelo, and she drew angels when she was a tiny child. She had curly, naturally blond hair and very green eyes. She was supposed to die when she did because she tried all her life to make her father understand that there is a God, and she did see angels and communicate with them. Her only purpose in her life was to paint in Italy and to bring the angels to life."

I stopped.

The father stared at me as if I were an alien.

The mother wept quietly.

Neither said a word.

The woman next to them waited patiently as I moved on to her. Her son's spirit was so strong I couldn't ignore him anymore.

Before the woman could ask a question, I said, "Your son was in the military. He died in the line of duty. He is here to tell you that the incident you experienced last night, in which you thought the man in the parking garage was following you, was not your imagination. He has followed you three times. He is stalking you. He intends to murder you and take your car. Do not go to the parking garage at night anymore without someone from work going with you. Inform the security people. They will find him lurking in the shadows."

I stopped. This information stunned even me. Many years ago I had gone through a period when I had received warning messages in my dreams or impressions and sometimes words from Mr. Voice, or from an angel, but usually I was the one being warned. It had been a very long time since this had happened.

The woman told me that everything I said was accurate. She had come to the meeting that night somehow knowing that her son was going to speak to her, but she didn't know how. She had received two warning dreams in which her son had come to her recently. Now she had real validation, she thought.

By the time the session had ended, every single parent had experienced a message or a visitation from his or her child without exception.

I was exhausted. I wondered how "mediums" and real psychics do this for a living! I was ready for a double cheeseburger.

We all said the Lord's Prayer in closing, and then the couples each asked me to sign their copies of my *Angel Watch* book. This was their chance to talk and hug me, which is the part I love the most.

The couple whose daughter went to Italy hung back until everyone was gone. The father wanted to thank me. He told me that he had truly fought coming to this session. His wife had been coming to the group for six months but this was his first time. He wanted me to know that just that afternoon, he had booked tickets to Italy for both of them to see Rome and all the places that had meant so much to their daughter; now their trip would take on a new meaning. Now they believed that their daughter had arranged this trip. In addition, their daughter was exactly as I had described physically, and she had painted . . . *angels.* Angel paintings hung all over their house.

"Now you know the real meaning of what an angel is. Your daughter was and is an angel."

I left the meeting, awed myself. When I got to my car I put my head on the steering wheel and thanked God for using me to help these people.

What I had not told any of these couples was that during one of the appearances of the children, I saw my own son. I heard his voice clearly say, "Hi, Mommy." I was and am now awed by the loving being that allows me to talk to Ethan, my little boy.

Epilogue: A week after this profound experience I went to Wednesday night Mass with my friend Fran. I told Fran about the experience and was surprised at her reaction.

"Catherine, how can you know this wasn't the work of the devil? What if everything you told them was evil? You need to talk to Father Vincente about this right away."

"Oh, Fran, if you were there, you would have felt all the love in that room. This was not a bad thing. But to make you happy, I will call Father Vincente and talk to him. If he says it's all okay, then will you not worry about me?"

"Yes."

The next day I called Father Vincente and set an appointment for the following Saturday morning.

Father Vincente was my priest at a Catholic church in downtown Houston that I loved very much. The church was built not long after World War I, and everything about the church, the facilities, the parishioners and the clergy here was special to me. This was my haven. One of my happiest memories was when I took my three-year-old granddaughter to this church and took her to a room behind the sacristy where she lit candles, gave an offering to the poor and we knelt on kneelers and said our prayers to Jesus.

Father Vincente was in his early seventies, yet still possessed an Italian accent from his early childhood in Italy. He met me at the door, and I brought him my favorite home-baked cookies to share with the other priests and a copy of my *Angel Watch* book. He was very appreciative, and then we sat down to talk.

I related my story to Father Vincente about the evening with the bereaved parents. I left nothing out of the story, but did not embellish either. I spoke to him of Fran's concern, and he listened very carefully. When I finished the story, he thumbed through my *Angel Watch* book, but didn't really read it. He just seemed to touch the pages and then closed the book, caught in a deep moment of reflection.

Without saying a word, he got up and went to the library

shelves in his office. He handed me a copy of *The Lives of the Saints*. In the Catholic Church, the saints are people who, in the past two thousand years, led exemplary lives. Some were tortured and killed for their faith. Others were deemed as saints because of their profound goodness and Christlike attitude toward their fellow man.

He asked me to read about St. Catherine. There are two St. Catherines. The first is St. Catherine of Alexandria who lived and died in the fourth century in Alexandria, Egypt. "She was a learned young girl of noble birth who protested the persecution of Christians under the Roman emperor Maxentius, and defeated the eminent scholars summoned by Maxentius to oppose her. The spiked wheel (whence the term Catherine wheel) by which she was sentenced to be killed broke, and she was then beheaded. She is the patron of philosophers and scholars" (*Encyclopaedia Britannica*, 15th edition).

St. Catherine was a mystic writer.

The second is St. Catherine of Siena who lived 1347 to 1380 and was a member of the Dominican Order. She is credited with returning the papacy (pope's rule) from Avignon to Rome in 1377. She is the patron saint of Italy.

"Catherine's writings, all of which were dictated, include about 380 letters, 26 prayers, and the four treatises of *Il libro della divina dottrina* ("The Dialogue of Saint Catherine"). The record of her ecstatic experiences in the *Dialogo* (circa 1475; modern English translation by A. L. Thorold, 1925) illustrates her doctrine of the 'inner cell' of the knowledge of God and of self into which she withdrew" (*Encyclopaedia*

Britannica, 15th edition). She was a mystic writer, just like the first St. Catherine.

I had studied the saints as a child in Catholic grade school. Obviously, their impressions on me were less than my favorite Grimm's fairy tales. Suddenly, I realized that the most interesting aspect about both these women was that they were mystics and writers. Translation: they talked to the angels.

After I read about each of the women, Father Vincente said to me, "All my life, I have prayed to be given this gift. I have asked God to give me what he gave St. Catherine, the patron saint of Italy."

Then he looked at me. "There is nothing here for you to be afraid of, Catherine. When God gave your son a genetic disease that caused his death at birth, he was giving you, at the same time, the chance to speak through this experience to those people who would suffer as you have suffered."

I stared at him without blinking. There was a long silence as I both savored and reflected on the moment.

"Father Vincente, I never told you that my son had a genetic disease and that he died at birth."

The startling truth overwhelmed both of us. I was covered in chills, but in a very good way. It was as if the angels were standing with us. Father Vincente's eyes filled with tears. He covered his face with his hands.

"I have had this gift all along? I have prayed for this. And I didn't know I had the gift."

"Father, you have been counseling human beings all your life. You have given your life to others. There is nothing but love in your every cell. Of course you have been speaking to the angels. You just needed a fine-tune adjustment in your translations is all."

We laughed and hugged that day, knowing that there was nothing special about us or even the saints Father Vincente had me read that day.

What was special was the love that we humans are able to convey to others to help them in their hour of need. That love was very great, indeed. We were simply the handmaidens of the divine.

Note: April 2005. I find it interesting that this experience has not happened to me or for me since this one time. That doesn't mean that it won't again. I do not profess to be a prophetess, psychic or mystic. I believe that it was a rare event and that I was "used" by the angels to bring solace to deeply grieving parents who needed answers, hope and proof that God loved them, even though their child had been taken from them. "God works in mysterious ways," I have been told. I truly believe that.

Angelic
Visitations
Nocturnal

hese angelic visitations are the ones we have all read about in the Bible, and quite frankly, nearly all religions have stories of angelic visitations during the sleep process.

Just as in the story of the angel who appeared to Joseph, telling him to take Mary and the baby, Jesus, into Egypt to avoid the slaughter of the innocents that was about to take place due to the edict by King Herod, nocturnal angelic visitations usually warn us about impending danger to us or someone in our family. What we don't know about Joseph's story is what the angel looked like. All we know are the words, "an angel of the Lord." We don't know if the angel had wings, dark hair, blond hair or any hair. The angel could have been a messenger appearing in human form.

For the purpose of this section, we will incorporate angels who appear in human dreams with wings and without.

We will also include stories that do not necessarily warn of danger, death or illness, but may simply come to comfort or even inform the human about some detail of his or her life.

It is also important to understand that the recipient of the visitation may or may not be actually dreaming. Though modern science and psychology would like to think that they know a great deal about the mind, brain and the dream state, the truth is, the brain alone is a fathomless abyss of unknown territory. We still don't really know how the brain works. We know even less about the mind, since the mind incorporates *emotions* and the *human will* into its thought processes. There is so little known about the dream state that I believe it is difficult to discern between what is a dream and what is an angelic or spiritual visitation.

The more science investigates the brain's ability to accomplish feats now termed "mediumship," "psychic ability," "remote viewing," "telepathy," "telekinesis" and related "supernatural" (above known nature) human abilities, the more validation we will have in the future that angelic visitations are real. They are part and parcel of the human experience.

Only thirty years ago, the general public did not know what microwaves were. We couldn't see them. We couldn't measure them. Today, an entire generation, such as my granddaughter, believes that "microwaves" are how you cook food. She doesn't know there was a time when food could not be heated instantly.

In the coming generations, we may finally be able to photograph or record angels in exactly the same way that we now record the voice of a departed soul or spirit on audiotape.

With special film, we can take photographs of human spirits who have long ago died. With special film and cameras, we can photograph and print images of the colors of the auras around each of our bodies. I like to think of these colors as the colors of our thoughts and emotions. Truly, if we think ill of others, we will be surrounded in muddy brown. If we think well of others and ourselves, we will be enveloped in happy yellows and bright hues of blue. If we keep our hearts focused on the angels, we will be cocooned in their glorious white and gold; thus, the "halos" around the angels, saints and Jesus Christ as depicted by the masters in their paintings and art.

This is free will. This is choice.

This also lends contemporary and scientific credence to "Do unto others as you would have them do unto you."

The *single most important criterion* about a nocturnal angelic visitation is that even though you believe it is a dream, *you never forget the experience.* To you, it is as real as any fully conscious reality you have experienced. Even decades later, the particulars of the "dream experience" become clearer. Every aspect, word, message and inference is remembered.

On the Sunny Algerian Beach

The Hair Factory is a small-town kind of beauty salon, plucked right out of a scene in *Steel Magnolias*, that exists in chic, glitzy Houston's Galleria area. The stylists, manicurists and shoe shiners are more family than merely coworkers. They have worked together for fifteen years or more to my knowledge. They have attended and helped to coordinate each others' weddings, children's graduations, baby showers and family funerals. They have lived in and out of each others' pockets for so long, it is no wonder my friend Vicki's coworkers often pop into her nocturnal dreams.

One of Vicki's fellow stylists is named Alice. Her daughter, Bernadette, was a manicurist at the Hair Factory until recently when she landed a job with a large Houston corporation. Bernadette is a favorite with Vicki, who is openly vocal about her love and concern for Bernadette.

On June 3, 2001, as Vicki was reading just before falling asleep, she found herself not in a dream but in a remote viewing situation. (I am including this story in this section because to many, this kind of incident is still deemed a "dream state.")

Remote viewing is the activation of our "psi abilities," an innate hardwiring in our brain that allows us to see or "be" in two places at one time. The U.S. military and U.S. intelligence agencies have used individuals who have trained and perfected this brain activity to such an extent that they can literally "see" into foreign offices, read documents and recite what they are reading. They can overhear conversations, see the participants in meetings and aid police and FBI investigations in tracking criminals and murderers. Remote viewing is not abnormal. It is a function of a highly evolved human brain.

In the generations to come, it won't be uncommon at all for humans to "visit" friends and relatives simply by "willing" themselves to another locale.

In this scenario, Vicki found herself standing on a beach in Algeria. Why she was there she hadn't the slightest idea. She didn't know anyone in Algeria. Or so she thought.

Still wearing the all-white, long nightgown she'd donned earlier that evening, Vicki walked along the beach until she came to what looked like a convenience store. There she saw none other than Bernadette's boyfriend, Salim, who indeed lived in Algeria!

She watched as Salim and two of his friends went into the convenience store. The place was small with rickety shelves, but there was a soda cooler, a rack of candy, a large display of cigarettes and many kinds of canned goods, household items, and magazines and newspapers much like one sees in the United States.

Salim went to the clerk and asked for two packs of cigarettes while his friends each bought sodas and iced drinks.

They took their drinks out to a grouping of very large, flat-topped rocks. Here they sat and gazed at the sunset.

"Salim, why don't you let me introduce you to my sister's friend?"

"No, thanks," Salim said, lighting his cigarette.

"But she's lovely, and you are always alone. It would be fun to have you come with all of us to supper or to the beach."

"How many times must I tell you, Hassim? I am very much in love with an American girl."

"This Bernadette?"

"Yes," Salim answered turning away from his friend.

"She must not love you very much. She is in America, and you are here. Why aren't you together?"

Sadness riddled Salim's eyes. "It pains me to speak of it. I am a torn man. I love Bernadette very much, but I cannot leave my Mimi."

"Mimi?"

"Yes. She is only three, and she needs me, too."

Vicki couldn't believe her ears. "Salim has a daughter?"

With that thought, Vicki found herself propelled back to Houston with a wwhhhooosh! She describes it as being very much like one of those camera pullback shots in a movie when the actor looks very tiny in the background one second and then in an instant moves to full size in the foreground. She was wide awake. She had not slept. She was still wearing her white gown.

The next morning at work, Vicki asked Alice, "Where is Salim right now?"

"Why, he's in Algeria."

Vicki felt those familiar goose bumps. "I don't mean to pry,

Alice, but I have to tell you about this incident I had last night."

"Were you remote viewing again?" Alice asked.

"Yes, I was."

Watching Vicki's dark eyes evade her, Alice pressed on. "And you saw Salim?"

"Yes, I did." Vicki then went on to tell her about the beach, his two friends and the flat rocks. But she held back.

"I don't like the look on your face, Vicki. Was he with another woman?"

"No. It wasn't that. But he did mention a three-year-old girl. Mimi. Does he have a daughter that Bernadette doesn't know about?"

"I have no idea," Alice replied with concern.

"Would you ask her to call Salim and ask him where he was last night? Tell her everything I've told you. I need validation that I was accurate in what I heard and saw."

"I'll do it right now," Alice said picking up the phone to call Bernadette.

That night when Bernadette phoned Salim at their appointed "date" time, she indeed asked him where he'd been the night previously.

"Why, I went to the beach with two of my friends."

"And what did you do there?" she asked.

"I bought two packs of cigarettes. Some drinks. Then Hassim and I talked for a bit. About you mostly. Why are you asking me these questions?"

"Salim, I know this will be difficult to understand, but my mother's friend Vicki says that she was remote viewing and she saw you last night at the beach. She said you mentioned a certain Mimi. I have to ask, Salim, is Mimi your daughter?"

Laughing, then suddenly stopping as the impact of all that Bernadette was saying hit him, Salim replied, "Mimi is my niece."

"Niece," Bernadette breathed easier.

"Yes, she's only three, blond hair, green eyes. Just a beautiful child. She adores me, and I miss her terribly when I'm in America. I keep thinking to myself that someday I'd like to have . . . well." His voice trailed off. "Bernadette, I met Vicki once at the shop, didn't I?"

"Yes, you did."

"My God! I had a dream about her last night. I dreamed she was dressed in a long white gown, and I said to her, 'Why are you here?' And she replied that she just wanted to know that I was well."

Gasping back her astonishment, Bernadette said, "Vicki told mother that she was wearing a long white nightgown as she stood on the beach. The same gown she wore to bed that night."

"And she overheard all of my conversation?"

"Yes."

"Then you will know how much I miss you and love you," Salim said.

"Yes, I do know that . . . more so now than ever before."

Bernadette and Salim said their good-byes. Bernadette then called Vicki to confirm all that she'd experienced in her remote viewing.

When Vicki told me this story she was still, over a week later, astonished at her own capabilities. She stated that in the past few weeks these occurrences were becoming more frequent. She also said that if this kind of thing was going to become part of her daily "routine" she would have to prepare herself.

"Prepare?" I asked. "By doing what?"

"Shopping, of course! I can't be going to beaches in Algeria dressed in an old rag like that!"

Revelations at Calgary

*E*ven from an angel's eye view, Calgary, Canada, is a ski lover's paradise. Arsenals of lush green pines blanket the slopes, ushering the eye downward to pristine glacier lakes and a welcoming valley community. Snowcapped Canadian Rocky Mountains stab crystal blue skies, reminding human spectators of the precariousness of our position in the universe. Timelessness pervades the area, and like all natural wonders, their very existence portends a need to reflect upon the meaning of our existence.

There is a uniqueness to these lesser populated natural sites of former cataclysms that lends a certain spiritual or otherworldly quality to them. Perhaps the fact that the Rocky Mountains were formed by cataclysmic upthrusts of the earth's plates, earthquakes, and the great and sudden arctic glacier that formed millions of years ago in the twinkling of an eye, freezing mastodons and ancient man for all time, may also have something to do with this pervasive surreal atmosphere.

It was in Calgary where my friend Vicki came face-to-once-living-face with one of her past lives.

Though Jim, her husband, was meeting with clients, the trip

for Vicki was a vacation. While Jim was busy during the day, Vicki took the opportunity to photograph the extraordinary scenery and browse the local art galleries and shops.

As she tells it, from her early childhood to adulthood she has always been fascinated with anything and everything Egyptian. Even as a child she wanted to someday visit the pyramids. The decor in her homes has always included profusions of marble, glass, pyramid shapes, desert colors of the golden Sahara and its sunsets.

One day during her stay in Calgary, she stumbled upon a small boutique that was filled with Egyptian treasures. Her immediate thought as she gazed at alabaster pyramid paperweights, tiny hand-carved wooden replicas of ancient Nile barges, pharaoh busts and hand-painted papyrus scrolls was that she needed more charge cards. This was where she intended to complete the bulk of her Christmas shopping.

After filling an entire shopping basket, she explained to the man behind the register that she needed another basket.

The dark-eyed man blinked at her, but did not respond.

"Don't you have another basket?" she asked.

The man simply stared at her.

Wondering if perhaps he didn't speak English, she said, "I'm sorry. We can just empty this one. I'll pay for these things and then continue shopping. Is that all right?"

The man finally snapped out of his trance. "Yes. Yes, My Lady. For you, anything!" He scrambled behind the counter and handed her another basket.

Eagle-eyed Vicki watched as he depressed a silent "call-button." She couldn't help but wonder what he was doing. Had she done something wrong? Was he calling for the police? Did he need assistance?

She looked around. There was no one else in the store. The hairs on the back of her neck stood on end. Something wasn't right. But what?

The man was quite tremulous, unsure of himself and without words as he fidgeted with her gift items. Curious, rather than frightened, she shook her head at his odd behavior and walked away.

From behind a row of hanging wind chimes and replicas of ancient Egyptian gods, Vicki peered at the man.

Clearly, he was staring at her with the same wide-eyed disbelief.

She was just about to march over to him and ask him to control his rudeness when the shop door opened and a second Egyptian man hurried inside and up to the counter.

"Where is she?" Vicki heard the second man ask. The man behind the counter pointed at Vicki.

With an audible gasp, the second man's eyes filled his face with amazement. And recognition.

Clamping his hand on each side of his face, his lips parted in an enormous grin.

"Am I missing something here?" Vicki said to herself.

The second man rushed toward her, the first man trailing behind.

"My Lady, you have come back to us!"

"Back . . . ?"

"We have waited so long for your return!" he cut her off with his enthusiastic outburst.

"You're mistaken. This is my first time in Calgary," she replied.

"I am Gamal. This is my brother, Hassim," the second man said.

As Hassim's expression settled from shock to delight, Vicki smiled at them, then frowned.

"Do I know you?" she asked politely.

"One would hope," Gamal said.

"But no, probably not," Hassim added.

"I don't understand. If I've never been to Calgary and we have never met, then how could you possibly know me?"

The brothers glanced at each other and chuckled, momentarily savoring their shared secret. Their faces solemn again, they stared intently at her.

"You don't know? You don't feel it?"

"It?"

"Something special, familiar about being here? With us? Our store?"

"I adore this store. You have beautiful things. . . ."

"Things you love?" Gamal interrupted.

"Why yes, of course. I've always been fascinated with Egypt."

"Always." Hassim jabbed his brother with his elbow, rocking back on his heels, as if satisfied with her answer.

Narrowing her eyes, Vicki's patience with their little game was growing thin. "I take it you liked my answer. Except that I still don't understand why that would please you. Now you owe me an answer. What did you mean when you said that I have returned to you?"

"Precisely what I said," Gamal replied placing his hand on her elbow. "Just turn around."

Vicki turned as she was instructed.

Suspended on the back wall in a place of honor was an enormous oil painting of herself.

As her blood turned to ice, it was Vicki's turn to feel the air freeze in her lungs. Time stood still. Then retrogressed.

She felt as if the earth fell out from under her, and she was alone in the universe facing this portrait. Thickly lashed, coal-black eyes stared at her out of her own heart-shaped face, framed with waves of hair.

The woman in the portrait wore a collar of gold links, emeralds, rubies, turquoise and onyx. Her hands crossed over her breast bearing the royal scepters and ankhs. On her head she wore a queen's headdress.

The woman was not young and therefore, Vicki surmised, this was the reason she was portrayed with gray hair, though Vicki's had been platinum from birth. But there was no mistaking the bone structure, the face and the confidence in those eyes. It was the same face Vicki saw in the mirror every morning.

"It can't be," Vicki said.

"It is you. Truly," Gamal replied.

"Who is she?"

"Nefiri," they replied in unison. "Our queen. Our Goddess. And she lives again!"

"Oh, no. I'm just Vicki. From Houston. I'm nobody's queen."

"Yes, you are. But you are in shock. In time, you will understand your purpose and why you have incarnated again. All will be revealed. My brother and I, we are honored that it was here, with us, that you have come to this divine awareness."

"All I wanted was Christmas presents for my family and

friends," she replied with a dry mouth.

"We have a gift for you," Hassim said and raced to the counter where he pulled out a lead crystal pyramid. Reverently he handed it to Vicki.

"I can't possibly accept this. It's too expensive," she said.

"You must take it. In remembrance of this moment."

Gamal smiled. "Not long from now, you will be given another sign, to remind you of us . . . and your past. Then you will know your mission. Your purpose."

"I don't know what to say, but thank you," she smiled.

"Perhaps a hug?" Hassim asked.

They laughed together as Vicki hugged them.

Vicki finished her shopping, and while Gamal rang up her purchases, she wandered back to the portrait, taking in its every detail.

Leaving the shop, she felt a divine shift take place inside her. If she'd ever doubted the concept of past lives before, that doubt was eliminated.

Like the tiny crystals in a kaleidoscope, the unanswered questions in Vicki's life finally began falling into spectacular grand design. The dreams she'd experienced all her life about a life in Egypt now made sense.

Loading her rented car and driving away, the question she asked now was, "How long until I discover my spiritual mission in my life?"

—To be continued in
"Bag of Pyramids"

Bag of Pyramids

here are no ancient pyramids in Los Angeles. Therefore, the last thing my friend Vicki ever thought she'd find while accompanying her sister, Pat, to Pat's annual company convention was any connection to Egypt or her phenomenal experience in Calgary, Canada, two years earlier.

In fact, the entire weekend had transformed into one disaster after another. Pat's husband was ill. Their mother had just been released from the hospital due to an ongoing frighteningly serious heart condition, and Vicki's daughter, Angela, was ill. The weather had turned gruesome in Los Angeles, and the airport had shut down. There was no way the women could return to Houston. They were stuck in Los Angeles. With all the family in Houston and the two sisters half a continent away, no one was resting well.

While Pat went to the convention, Vicki made another round of phone calls to Houston, to assure herself everyone was at least status quo. She decided to kill a couple of hours shopping and then meet Pat for lunch. Because her mind was on the situation at home, Vicki's shopping consisted of mindless browsing. She found herself in a gift store filled with items from local artisans. Nothing intrigued her except for a group of turquoise, crystal and alabaster pyramid shapes.

She bought a half dozen pyramids in various sizes and colors. Vicki chatted with the shopgirl while she rang up her purchases.

"These are very delicate," the girl said. "I'll triple wrap them in tissue for your trip back to Texas. In fact, I have a nice velvet bag we can put them in."

"Oh, I don't need anything that special. Paper will do."

"It's okay. It's a promotional item left over from an event we had six months ago. It's not a problem."

"Thank you. That would be wonderful."

"It's got our logo on it. Then you'll always remember today," the girl said cheerily.

Those last words made goose bumps crawl over Vicki's arms. *Where have I heard someone say that to me before?* she wondered, not thinking of Calgary. Because it was a common enough statement, Vicki didn't pay attention. She took the bag, paid the girl and left.

Vicki then met Pat for lunch, and for the umpteenth time telephoned Houston to check on everyone.

Riddled with concern, Vicki convinced Pat that perhaps they could drive to San Jose or even San Francisco and try to fly home out of another airport. Pat agreed. But when Vicki called for the flights, the earliest they could get was the following morning at the crack of dawn. Circumstances were making another night in Los Angeles a certainty.

Vicki battled sleeplessness for hours as her fears pressed upon her like banshees. Not until one in the morning did she finally fall asleep. The last thought she had as she drifted off was of the bag of pyramids sitting atop her already packed suitcase. She whispered a prayer for her husband, Jim, and fell into slumber.

At five in the morning, Vicki's cellular phone rang. Vicki bolted awake, certain that the worst had happened. "Mother? Angela? Who . . . is there? What has happened?"

"Vicki?"

"Yes, Jim. What is it? Who's in trouble?"

"No one. Um, you . . . you're still in Los Angeles?" he asked.

"Of course, I'm still here."

"How can that be?" Dismay rattled through Jim's voice.

"Because we can't get a flight until seven, Jim. But I already told you that."

"I know. I know," he replied, unconvinced.

"Jim, what is it? You sound . . . strange. Are you all right?"

"Vicki, I have to ask you. How could you be in two places at once?" he asked.

It was her turn to be confused. "You are making no sense . . ."

Before she could finish, Jim cut in, "I saw you, Vicki. Last night. I saw you standing next to our bed. You were holding a bag of pyramids. You woke me up. I asked you what you were doing there, and you said, 'I wanted to make sure you were all right.'"

"A bag of pyramids?" she questioned hesitantly.

"Yes."

"Jim, I bought some pyramid paperweights for gifts today. They are in a velvet bag," she said pointing across the room as if he could see the bag long distance.

"The bag was velvet. Black velvet. Yes, I'm sure of it," he replied.

"You couldn't have known that," she said. "This is too weird. It was just a dream, Jim."

"Not this time. I touched you, Vicki! It was real. You were real. You touched my hand. I felt flesh. The real you! I was wide-awake. I looked at the clock. It was three in the morning. That is one o'clock your time."

"This isn't happening," she whispered wiping her hand over her eyes.

"Vicki, I don't know how you did it, but you did."

"What are you saying to me, Jim?"

"That you were obviously in two places at once."

"I was praying for you, Jim. For our whole family."

"I swear to you, Vicki, I will make you a promise. I will never, ever doubt your powers again. I . . . I called just to tell you that."

"After twenty years of marriage . . ." she marveled, "you make this promise now?"

"I'll never doubt again," he said. "Maybe there was something to that incident in Calgary years ago. All I know is . . . I love you."

"I love you, too," she said.

"I'll pick you up at the airport. Bye for now," he said and hung up.

At that moment, Vicki's mind was catapulted back to that afternoon in Calgary. "You will see your divinity. You will be shown your divine mission," Gamal had said.

Flying back to Houston, Vicki prayed for the health of all her family members. Before the last prayer escaped her lips, a flood of reassurance enveloped her. Somehow, she knew that everyone was safe from harm's way. Life would go on.

When Vicki landed, Jim was there waiting with open arms. He told her that everyone, including her mother, had experienced a miraculous turnaround.

Vicki's spiritual mission hit her full force. Her job on earth was what it had always been, and was one from which she had never wavered . . . to love and heal her family and friends through prayer and with God at her side. It was and is the noblest of missions.

Roses Are Red, Roses Are Pink

My sister, Nancy, has a lot going on. I think of all the people I know, and few can juggle as many situations, crises, business decisions and "adjustments to schedules" as Nancy does. Mother says that the Energizer Bunny's original battery started in Nancy, only hers is still going and going.

Twelve years ago Nancy invented a line of spectacular jams called "Nanny Jams." Though the product was fabulous, the sales were not. Lack of personnel (only Nancy) to make the jam; lack of office managers (only Nancy) to balance the books; and lack of sales personnel (only Nancy) to sell the jam caused Nancy to redirect her business from the jam to corporate baskets in which she could place the jam.

From that point, she opened a retail store, Celebrations To Go, and sold gift items. Again, she needed to redirect. She began a wedding registry complete with china and silver. A few years later she went to "Balloon Art School" and sold voluminous balloon designs worthy of a Venetian Renaissance artist. The call for her balloons brought in more brides. The brides then wanted Nancy to do with flowers what she'd accomplished with balloons. Nancy went to floral design school.

This led her to buying an eighteen-foot cooler for the roses she imported from Ecuador. As of this writing, Nancy is a full-fledged wedding planner, minus the Jennifer Lopez–styled dress! She coordinates every flower from prewedding showers to the church to the reception and includes the balloon art at the reception hall, the table decorations, linens, favors and chair covers. This coming weekend she has seven weddings on her plate. Her staff of five is hardly enough to take the load off her shoulders.

When Mother called to tell me about this particular dream Nancy had only days ago, I was astonished.

"She sleeps? When does she have the time for this?" I asked.

With a great deal of work and several meetings, Nancy landed the largest and most expensive wedding of the summer. She was thrilled with her accomplishment. She knew every detail had to be perfect. Three weeks prior to the wedding, Nancy consulted with the bride about the bouquets and last-minute touches to the table centerpieces and church flowers. The order for a soft shell-pink rose had been placed directly to Ecuador. The shipper assured Nancy that this very specific color rose was in plentiful supply and that though the order was inordinately large, they would be able to fill it.

Nan breathed a sigh of relief.

When I spoke with Nan the week before the wedding, she was excited about the designs she'd sketched and the innovations she'd planned to surprise the bride. The elegance of cream roses mingled with the shell-pink roses and huge calla lilies was nothing short of romantic drama.

Early on Thursday morning prior to the Saturday wedding, Nan awoke from a dream covered in cold goose bumps.

In the dream the shipper had telephoned her that her shipment of dozens and dozens of *shocking pink* roses had been shipped to her. In the dream she stood in the church, drowning in the wrong color roses. The bride was in tears. The mother of the bride was angry. It was a nightmare for her business.

"That can't be! I specifically ordered shell pink. A soft, soft blush pink. Shocking pink will ruin everything!"

Nancy flew out of bed that morning at six.

"Dave, wake up!" she said, nudging her husband awake.

"What's the matter?" he mumbled.

"I have to leave immediately for Chicago."

"Why?"

Nancy scrambled out of bed, grabbed a pair of jeans and started dressing. She whipped a headband into her hair and raced to the bathroom for her toothbrush, grabbing her purse on the way. "I have to talk to the shipper. There's some kind of mistake about my pink roses for the wedding on Saturday."

"Mistake?" Dave rubbed his eyes. "What kind of mistake?"

"He's sending me shocking pink roses. I need shell pink."

"There's a difference?" Dave asked opening his eyes fully.

"Don't ask, Dave." Nancy flew around the room as Dave watched her.

"It can't be that big of a deal."

"It is! Trust me!" She jammed her feet into her shoes. She headed for the door, then turned back to blow him a kiss. "Bye. I'll be back by noon."

"Aren't you even going to take a shower?"

"I don't have time."

"But you always take a shower."

"Not today."

Suddenly, Dave sat bolt upright. "Hey, Nan. How do you know they have the wrong shipment? When did they call?"

"They didn't call."

"Then how do you know?"

"I saw it in my dream."

"Yeah, right," Dave answered closing his eyes and lying back down. "See you at noon."

Nancy raced out of the house and drove out the driveway. Because it was so early, few cars were on the road. It's approximately one hour to Chicago from our hometown. Depending on where you have to go, it can take up to two hours if the destination is on the north side. Fortunately for Nancy, she was headed for midtown.

She arrived at the shippers at seven thirty, just after they'd opened their doors.

"I have to talk to the sales supervisor," Nan said rushing up to a dock man.

"You're in luck. She just got here and is leaving for vacation in an hour."

Nan went inside and found the woman who had taken her rose order weeks earlier.

"Nan, what are you doing here?" Anna asked.

"I have a feeling there's a mistake on my rose order for tomorrow. I want to double-check." Reaching into her pocket, Nan withdrew a swatch of the bridesmaids' dress fabric. "The roses need to match this color."

Anna flipped through her files and found Nancy's order. "This order is for Passion Roses. They're shocking pink."

"Shocking pink," Nancy's voice trembled. Then her hand shook. "Just like in the dream."

"The dream?"

Nan took a deep breath. "I had a dream last night that my rose order was not right. It's imperative the colors match. I ordered soft shell-pink roses. It's the biggest order I've ever placed with you. I have to get it right."

"I understand. But what I don't understand is how I got this wrong in the first place. That's not like me."

Anna scanned the colors of roses on her computer and found the error. "Shell-pink roses are called Paradise Rose. The shocking are called Passion Rose. On the list they are right above one another. No wonder they got confused. Or I did."

"It's a wonder all right," Nan replied.

It was Anna's turn to feel the goose bumps on the back of her neck. "You say you saw this mistake in a dream?"

"Yes."

"And you drove here at six in the morning from Indiana because you saw this in a dream?"

"Yes."

Anna shook her head. "Wow. That's some angel."

"Yeah, I'm lucky."

"Blessed, I'd say," Anna replied and went back to the computer. She corrected the mistake and made certain Nan's roses would arrive on time and be the right color.

"Thanks, Anna. I really appreciate this," Nan said shaking her hand and turning to leave.

"Nan. One thing."

"What's that?"

"Do you know where I can get one of those angels like you've got?" Anna asked with a broad smile.

"Sure."

"Where?"

"Just believe. Then pay attention."

This incident took place in La Porte, Indiana, May 30, 2001.

Dorothy's Asparagus Dream

AUTHOR'S NOTE: *This story was told to me by my mother, Dorothy Lanigan, on June 7, 2001.*

My nephew Ben graduated from high school June 2001. My sister Nan and her husband, Dave, decided to have a family graduation party at home on Saturday night.

Ben has always been a pride and joy to our family, but this year as a senior at La Porte High School, he reached his zenith. Participating in wrestling and track, Ben reached his all-time personal best in shot put this spring and took his team to State. Every week there was a new track meet. Every week, I got reports of Ben's triumph. Our proverbial "Family Pride" buttons were pinned to our chests.

When Ben went to Regionals, we all held our breaths until Mother called my brothers and me to tell us that Ben had won. The following week when Ben went to State, everything seemed to go wrong. The entire La Porte team was off. None of the team members performed like they had all season. Nan said it was as if Murphy's Law was working overtime against our team.

Ben's deflation was evident. To make up for this bummer of a mood, Nan wanted Ben's graduation party to be very special.

Nan marshaled all the kids, Ben, Elaine and Sam, to move all the furniture out of the living room and dining room. She wanted a sit-down dinner for all her guests. She covered the tables in snowy white linen, then ran wide orange and black satin ribbons (the La Porte High School colors) down the center. Interspersed with glowing gold votive candles were frosted votive holders with orange roses. Outside she festooned the yard with orange and black balloons and baskets of flowers on the back deck.

Nan's mother-in-law, Dureen, is the world's best pie baker. I defy anyone to make a better pie. Dureen grew up with parents who ran a bakery, and every morning as a young girl, it was Dureen's job to bake a dozen pies before going to school. On-the-job-training like that is priceless. Now in her eighties, Dureen has had ample opportunity to perfect even a tiny flaw. Personally, I would fly to Indiana *just* to get one of these pies. Dureen brought three strawberry pies and three blueberry pies to add to the two beef tenders Ben grilled on the grill, the spiral cut honey-baked ham and a pork tender. Mother contributed marinated asparagus.

In our hometown of La Porte, next to the red stone turn-of-the-last-century courthouse built in 1893 in the center of town, is a farmer's market every Saturday morning. Mother loves this market where the local farmers bring their freshest and best crops in bushel baskets and sell their items right off the back of their pickup trucks.

Mother rises at six on Saturdays to drive her fourteen-year-old Lincoln to the makeshift market to select the very best produce. Over the years, Mother has come to know many of these growers as most of them have small farms and, as a general rule, are about her vintage. They exchange stories and catch up on each others' children's lives in the process of shopping. Several of these farmers have been Mother's friends for decades. Some were clients of my father's when I was a child. Therefore, it is not unusual that Mother would have many of their telephone numbers in her address book.

On Wednesday night, June 6, the same night that Nan had her dream about the shocking pink roses (see "Roses Are Red, Roses Are Pink"), Mother had the same kind of precognitive dream.

In the dream, Mother was standing at the farmer's market, and her friend, Mrs. Burek, was telling her that there was no asparagus.

"There has to be asparagus. It's Ben's favorite vegetable. And it's his graduation dinner! It's going to be an elegant event. I have to have asparagus," Mother said.

"I'm sorry, Mrs. Lanigan, but the rain has been so intense this spring that the asparagus crops are miniscule. There just wasn't any this week."

Mother awoke with a start. Sitting up in bed she put her hand to her cool cheek. "It was so real! My dream was so very real!"

She got out of bed, made her coffee and found her address book with Mrs. Burek's number. Though it was early, she knew Mrs. Burek was up at the crack of dawn just as she was. She phoned her immediately.

The phone was picked up on the fourth ring. "Mrs. Burek, this is Dot Lanigan," Mother said.

"How are you today?" Mrs. Burek inquired.

"I'm fine, but I was wondering if you'll have asparagus at

the farmer's market on Saturday."

"I'm sorry to say, I won't. The weather has just been terrible for asparagus this year. I have some today, but it will all be gone by midmorning, Dot."

Mother felt goose bumps shiver down her spine. "My dream was right!"

"Dream?"

"I dreamed you were out of asparagus, Mrs. Burek, and everyone knows yours is the best. It's Ben's graduation dinner this Saturday and I promised my grandson I'd bring his favorite marinated asparagus."

"Did this dream tell you I have plenty of asparagus today?"

"Well, I guess so. That's why I'm calling. I'll drive out to your house to pick it up."

"How much do you need?

"Enough for twenty-five people."

"That's just how much I have, Dot," Mrs. Burek could not hide the astonishment in her voice.

"I can be dressed and out there in an hour or so. Just don't sell it to anyone else."

"Dorothy Lanigan! How could you think I would do such a thing? After all, you had angels telling you that this batch of asparagus was meant for your grandson."

"I guess I did at that!"

"I never thought I'd see the day," Mrs. Burek mused.

"What day?" Mother asked.

"The day that my asparagus was heaven-sent."

"But, Mrs. Burek. Everything we have is heaven-sent, isn't it?" Mother replied.

"Yes, it is, Dot. Yes, it absolutely is."

Sally in the Sand

F or those who do not understand past-life regressions and are seeking a clear-cut method of how to accomplish this kind of "altered-experience," I suggest consulting the book by Raymond A. Moody, Jr., entitled *Coming Back: A Psychiatrist Explores Past-Life Journeys.*

Sally was thirty-six years old when she and I used the relaxation method of regressing her to a past life. Sally was in the midst of a divorce and was searching for answers to the myriad of emotions she was experiencing. Her life had seemingly turned topsy-turvy, and though she said, like most people, often do, "This has been coming on for a long time," putting reason to chaos sometimes isn't enough.

She wanted more. She believed there was more to the fractured portrait of her life.

After lying on the sofa, Sally simply closed her eyes, and we began a countdown of simple relaxation techniques. In fact, we both thought aloud, "This is too easy. This can't be all there is to it." Indeed it was.

After relaxing her head, shoulders, arms, torso and legs, I read from the pages of Dr. Moody's book. Sally imagined herself rising above the earth and coming down in one of her past lives that would help her to understand the present. She would be able to see scenes in her past life and then move in and out of them at will. She would be totally conscious, able to talk about the actions and dialogues. If any particular sequence became too emotional, she could disengage from it, observe it and report on it.

Later, upon waking, she would remember everything she saw and experienced, and analyze and critique her own life as if it had happened to someone else.

"Do you see yourself hovering over the earth?" I asked Sally.

"Yes. It's beautiful here, above the clouds with only stars over my head."

"I want you to look down at earth and then start floating back to the blue planet. Down, down, you float. You are comfortable and safe, going at your own speed. When you reach earth you will land in a past lifetime that has particular significance to your life right now. Do you see yourself on earth yet?"

"Yes," she said, her eyes darting from right to left behind closed eyelids.

"Look at your feet. What kind of shoes are you wearing?"

"None. My feet are bare. I'm running across the sand. I stop. I see a horse. It's not my horse. It belongs to someone else. I know it's wrong to steal the horse. They will kill me for horse stealing."

"Do you know where you are?"

"In the desert," Sally answered.

"The American desert?"

"No. I've never heard of America. I've heard of

Mesopotamia. That's as far away as I've heard of another country."

"Where do you live?"

"That's what I'm trying to do . . . to get back to my home in Petra."

"Petra? Are you sure that's the name of your city?"

"Petra, yes." Sally was adamant about the name, though I'd never heard of it.

"Is there anything else you need to tell me?" I asked.

"My name is Mabooka."

"Interesting."

"I am running away from some men," Sally said. "One of them is my captor. He wants to make me his slave."

"Who is he?" I asked.

"Oh, no!" Sally gasped and opened her eyes. She sat bolt upright.

"What's wrong?" I asked her.

"I saw him, clear as a bell! It was my husband!" Clasping her hands on either side of her face she stared wide-eyed at me. "No wonder I want a divorce. Marriage to him is like enslavement!"

"This explains a great deal about these strange emotions you've been having," I ascertained.

"Do you think it's real?" Sally said. "I've never done anything like this. What if it's just a dream?"

"There's one way to find out, and that is to check the facts."

"What facts? We don't have any," Sally offered.

"Yes we do. If it's just a dream, there will be no such place as Petra."

"And how do we check that out?"

"Simple. My encyclopedia."

We scrambled up the stairs to my study and yanked a volume of the *Encyclopaedia Britannica* from the shelves. The following is the exact wording for the description of Petra:

Petra. Arabic Batra, an ancient city, center of an Arab Kingdom in Hellenistic and Roman times; its ruins are in Ma'an *muhafazah* (governorate) Jordan. The city was built on a terrace, pierced from east to west by the Wadi Musa (the Valley of Moses) one of the places where, according to tradition, the Israelite leader Moses struck a rock and water gushed forth. The valley is enclosed by sandstone cliffs veined with shades of red and purple varying to pale yellow; and for this reason Petra is often called the "rose-red city."

The Greek name Petra (rock) probably replaced the biblical name Sela. The site is usually approached from the east by a narrow gorge known as the Sik (Wadi as-Sik) one and one-fourth miles long. Remains from the Paleolithic and the Neolithic periods have been discovered at Petra, but little is known about the site up to c. 312 BC, when the Nabataeans, an Arab tribe, occupied it and made it the capital of their kingdom. Under their rule, the city prospered as a center of the spice trade.

When the Nabataeans were defeated by the Romans in AD 106 Petra became part of the Roman province of Arabia but continued to flourish until changing trade routes caused its gradual commercial decline. After the Islamic invasion in the 7th century, it disappeared from history until it was finally rediscovered by the Swiss traveler John Lewis Burckhardt in 1812.

Excavations from 1958 onward on behalf of the British School of Archaeology in Jerusalem and the American School of Oriental Research have added considerably to knowledge of pre-Roman Petra. Al-Khaznah, one of the many rock-cut monuments, has an impressive columned facade and probably dates from the 2nd century AD. The most noteworthy feature of Petra are the tombs, often with elaborate facades and now used as dwelling places.

After reading this information, Sally was convinced that her mind was able to access parts of her past that she'd never before known existed. She was ready to embark on a second past-life regression.

The next time, Sally relaxed into the meditation with ease.

Again she saw herself floating above her body, above the room, above the house, into the sky, then into the clouds and finally space. Slowly she descended. She came to earth and again found her bare feet in the sand.

"My feet are in the sand . . . again!" Sally said with closed eyes.

"Is there anything different from the last time?"

"Yes. I know I'm not Mabooka. I don't know who I am this time. Maybe I don't have a name. We are walking. My feet are bare, except for the chain around my ankles."

"Chains? Why chains?"

"I am a slave. The traders have us all chained to another so we won't run away. They are so stupid. Why would any of us run? Everyone knows no one escapes the desert."

"That's true," I said.

"Oh, now I see why we are chained. There is a river. I don't know what river it is. Some said it is the Jordan. But I do not know this. The men who are moving us are riding on horses and camels. They have elaborate reins for their animals. In fact their animals are treated with respect. We are not."

"What else can you tell me?" I asked.

"The sand is so hot. If I ever live through this, someday I will have shoes to protect my feet. Like the traders. They have exquisite boots. I envy these men their shoes more than their food. My feet are blistered and bloody from the sand. I long to cool them in the river, but if I break the line, they will kill me."

"Is there anything else you need to learn from this lifetime?" I asked her.

"I will never be a slave again to any man. Ever. This I vow to myself."

Slowly, I brought Sally up out of the regression, she moved back up to heaven and this time floated down into her body, which was alive and well in the present time. She woke refreshed and enlightened.

"My God, I think one of the traders was my husband again. Is that possible? That he always owned me? That I was always his slave? No wonder I feel resentment! And my feet! I can nearly feel them burning and the pain."

"I found that particularly interesting. Think about the current-life shoe fetish you have. I don't know anyone with as many kinds and styles of shoes as you!"

We both laughed aloud.

"That's true! How interesting to finally understand myself in this way!" Reflexively, she rubbed her stockinged feet even though they had never set foot in a desert in this current life.

"Boy, from now on, I'm never, ever going to feel guilty about a new pair of shoes. I've earned every pair from my Keds to my satin bedroom slippers!"

"Amen to that!" I said hugging her.

For many, past-life regressions may seem like hocus-pocus or silliness. But for those who put their earnestness into the process, if it serves only to access some part of our cell memory that does indeed perform the function of psycho-analysis, then only positive insights will be gleaned from the experience.

To be able to see one's life from a new perspective and then in turn to alter the paradigm of your life to create a better understanding, isn't this precisely what we would all want for ourselves? To put our guilt, shame and dilemmas to rest is a blessing. Only then can one proceed to the future with an open mind, a more loving heart and a helping hand to others.

Grandma at My Bedside

he only time I remember my Grandmother Ethel being at my bedside was after she'd been dead for a week. I've never really known why she chose me to visit once she'd crossed over. I have no recollection of my being any particular favorite grandchild of hers. Truth be known, my cousin Barb was probably Grandma's favorite. Barb loved horses, and Grandma and Grandpa had a ranch in northwestern Florida for years; they had many horses there. I never rode horses in Florida, though I remember seeing my grandfather ride them. We lived a thousand miles away in La Porte, Indiana, and I was quite young when he died, therefore the opportunity did not present itself.

My cousins, Barb and Beth, grew up in a small town near my Grandmother Ethel, so they were the ones with whom she was most likely to bond. They went to church together, celebrated more holidays together, and were in and out of each others' houses and lives on a weekly, if not daily, basis. For my grandmother to choose to visit me, not even my mother, or either of her two sons, seems the least bit odd.

My grandmother's funeral was conducted in much the same way as my Grandfather Clyde's had been six years earlier—in the Southern tradition. This meant that the body was laid out in a casket in the front "parlor" of the house. Because my family was visiting from Indiana, we did not stay in a hotel or motel. We remained in the house, each occupying the various bedrooms.

At the time I was thirteen. My days of childhood "imaginings" were far behind me, so my mother told me. She did this so that I would be strong and fearless for my younger brothers and sister. Mother's duties of greeting guests, mourners and incoming family from the surrounding Southern states kept her exhausted from predawn till dusk. My father, being an attorney, was executor of the estate, and there was a great deal for him to oversee. Neither had a smidge of time to spend with their children.

This left the explanation of the dead body in the living room up to me.

"This is just too creepy," my year-younger brother, Ed, declared, staring down at my grandmother's lifeless body.

"They did the same thing when Grandpa died," I informed him.

"I don't remember it. I was too young," Ed said.

"She was never really even sick," my sister, Nancy, said. "How do we know she's really dead?"

"She's been in a casket for two days. She's dead, all right," Ed replied authoritatively.

"I thought we were supposed to be praying now," Nancy questioned, looking up at me.

"Not till we get to the church," I answered, not knowing if my grandmother's Presbyterian rules were the same as Catholic rules.

"I like the funeral homes in Indiana better," Ed said finally. "You can come and go when you want, and you don't have to sleep with the body."

"What if Grandma wakes up and comes into our room tonight?" Nancy asked, fear filling her face.

"She can't wake up!" Ed exclaimed. "The only time the dead can get up is after they are a skeleton, and that takes years before their flesh rots off. I should know. I'm going to be a doctor. You have to know stuff like that in medicine."

"Skeletons scare me," Nancy shivered.

I flashed Ed a glaring look. "He's kidding, Nancy. He was just trying to scare you."

Nancy balled her tiny fist and punched his arm. It had no impact. Ed was a tough guy. He flicked off her blow with his hand and left the room. He'd had enough fun at our expense.

"So, can dead people walk?" Nancy asked me somberly.

"No," I replied with all the authority I could conjure. "Once you're dead, you fly. All the way to heaven."

Nancy was relieved. "Wings. Yes. Like angels," she mused happily. "It's nice to think of Grandma with wings."

As Nancy left the room to get some lemonade in the kitchen, I couldn't help wondering why Grandma with wings didn't ring true for me. Little did I know that in less than a week I'd have my answer.

The funeral over, the furnishings, the silver, crystal, china and linens divided, we packed up my mother's heirlooms and treasures in a U-Haul and headed back to Indiana. It was a somber drive home for my mother, but I remember her strength, making plans for the future for the rest of the school season and for the upcoming trip back to Florida for us kids that summer. Grandma was gone, but life went on.

We were back in Indiana only two nights when I had a dream that I saw Grandma Ethel walking across a map of the United States from Florida to Indiana. She walked across the state of Indiana, then I saw her walking across the golf course in front of our house, up the front yard to the door and into the house. She came down the hall and into my bedroom. I could hear Nancy's voice asking that question again. "Do dead people walk?"

Terrified, I woke up with a scream.

Sitting bolt upright, I was no longer asleep, but very much awake.

There, standing at the end of my twin bed, was Grandma. I trembled, I was so afraid. I'd never seen a ghost before.

"Cathy, wake up."

"I'm awake," I said hesitantly. I remember distinctly touching the blanket to make sure I was not sleeping. I pulled it around me like armor.

"Don't be afraid."

"Well, I *am* afraid, Grandma. You're supposed to be dead."

"I am dead to your world. But not to mine."

"There's a difference?"

"I came to tell you something. You have to promise me that you will always remember."

"I will."

"Always and forever," she said very firmly.

"I will. I promise," I said.

"First, I want you to tell your mother that you saw me. Tell her that I love her."

"That's easy. She knows that."

"No, she doesn't, but you have to be the one to tell her."

"Why me?"

"Because you have always been the mother. She is the daughter."

"Grandma, something must have happened to your memory when you died. I am the daughter."

"You'll understand later."

I shook my head thinking, "Boy, even dead she treats me like a child."

Then she grew very serious, but I also noticed that she seemed to be fading. Her body was becoming transparent, and I could see the sliding closet doors right through her!

"I want you to write my story someday."

"What story?"

"The story of my life."

"Why would I do that, Grandma? I'm not a writer."

"But you will be. That's what I'm here to tell you. It's your destiny. You will be a writer when you grow up."

Then she vanished.

Not a word of good-bye, no awesome information about Jesus or my guardian angel. Nothing. I was so disappointed; I couldn't believe she left me in a lurch like that.

I remember still being terrified that this ghost had come to see me. What if the devil had sent it? What if it was a trick? What if she wasn't really my grandma? And what was all that stuff about being the mother when I was only thirteen and my mother was, after all, my mother?

The next morning during breakfast I told my mother about the dream. She was so busy making lunches, packing our lunch boxes, counting out milk money, getting my little brother dressed and answering my father's calls about the location of his navy blue socks, that she didn't really hear what I was saying.

"It wasn't a dream," I said adamantly. "I was awake."

"I'm sure you were. I'm sure she was there," my mother replied with so little concern, I couldn't help wondering just how many dead relatives had turned up at her bedside during her life?

"What did she mean, I was the mother and you were the daughter?" I asked.

"You just probably heard her wrong."

This was the kind of answer I could deal with. "That's it. I'm remembering it wrong."

"Of course, dear. Now hurry up, your father's backing the car out of the garage to drive you all to school."

That was that. Discussion closed.

The only thing wrong with this scenario is that the words of that "visitation" have been imbedded in my memory bank all these years. They are words I would swear were only spoken yesterday. As my life has fast-forwarded and I have accomplished precisely what Grandma Ethel foretold I would, to become a writer and write her "story," the other words of her missive have even greater meaning for those of you reading this story today.

Several years ago when I decided to compile these stories into my first *Angel Watch* book, I was talking with my mother about Grandma's visit. Going over every single statement Grandma's spirit had said, my mother brought to my attention something I had never known.

"I've never told you this, but when Mother was dying,

she and I were not exactly on the best of terms. That's why I discounted your statement that she said to tell me that she loved me," my mother said. "There had always been a difference of opinion between my mother and me about your father, Cath. Ethel never liked him because he was Catholic. She never forgave me for marrying him. On her deathbed she asked me to promise her that I would leave him. I told her I would never promise that. I got up and left. She died not long after that."

This confession of my mother's makes that statement, "Tell your mother I love her," incredibly poignant. Truly one can hear the apology ringing across the barriers of time. Maybe this was the reason Grandma came to visit me and used me to relay her message.

Regarding her other statements, years of study, experience and exposure to esoteric knowledge has led me to the belief that when my grandmother's ghost visited me a week after her death, her simple statement of "You have always been the mother. She is the daughter," coming from the Other Side, is a direct reference to past incarnations, past lives.

On this side of the Veil, we can only see this earthly reality. Our ancestors, relatives and departed friends and even angels on the Other Side do "visit" us in dreams and sometimes in waking moments. Their brief statements may not seem important or even have impact at the time, but they are.

It is our duty, once we begin our "angel watch," to carefully pay attention to these divine nudges. Rather than be terrified at seeing a "spirit" or "ghost," we should commit their every phrase to memory. Because I was so young at the time, even if I had not consciously made an effort to remember her every word, I did in my naïveté, simply because I thought she'd lost her marbles! I was nearly making fun of how Grandma had gotten things so mixed up! It wasn't until I had experienced my own past lives through regression, dèjá vu, dreams and dream therapy, even some tangible evidence, that I realized my own grandmother had been there since I was thirteen, constantly guiding me and imparting information that was vital not just to me, but to those who would someday read my words.

I also found it interesting that she used the word "destiny." She had told me that it was my "destiny" to become a writer when I grew up. When my father died, and five years earlier when he had his first near-death experience he, too, made statements about my "destiny" after returning from the Other Side. Both people told me exactly the same thing. What is interesting to me today, as of this writing, is that twenty years ago, I wrote a novel called *Maybe Someday*. It was my grandmother's story, complete with historical references given to me by my mother. However, the story never sold. I don't even know if I still have the five-hundred-page manuscript around anymore after all these years, all my moves and many houses. Perhaps that is not the story my grandmother wanted me to tell. Perhaps *this* is the story she meant. Perhaps this "spiritual visitation" of hers is the most important story of her life, of her afterlife.

The goose bumps on my arms and legs confirm it. It took me exactly forty years to figure out what she was saying and what she wanted me to do. With this writing, April 16, 2005, I believe that Grandma is finally pleased.

A Phone Call from Fran

 wo of my parents' best friends were Fran and Al Rumely. The Rumelys lived in an enormous three-story house on majestic Michigan Avenue in La Porte. I have always loved that house with its big square kitchen surrounded with white painted cabinets with clear glass doors allowing me to peek inside at Fran's beautiful china.

Theirs was the only house I'd been in that had a vestibule, a reception area, and *then* a living room. Most of our neighbors lived in brand-new ranch houses where the front door opened directly into a living room. But the Rumelys had honest-to-goodness receiving areas. There was a huge staircase that swept up to the second floor where all the girls' bedrooms were located. The third floor was off-limits to all girls and that included Lanigan girls especially. Theirs was the only household in which one night a week, Wednesday nights as I remember, no one was allowed to speak English at the dinner table. French was the only accepted mode of verbal exchange. In contrast, my father taught us German beer songs.

There were seven Rumely children and four Lanigan children. Each of the Lanigans had a Rumely child in our grade school classrooms. Our fathers were on the parish board of trustees, our mothers in the same rosary circles and church societies. When they were young they sewed their daughters' dresses, and later Fran and Mother began crewel and needle-point together. Later in her life, Fran went so far as to design patterns and then conduct classes in needlepoint.

The two couples played bridge and golf and hosted parties together. Rumely and Lanigan girls all went to Brownies and Girl Scouts together and boys played on the same parochial football teams. It would have been very difficult to go through life in La Porte without banging into a Lanigan or Rumely somewhere along the line.

For thirty years or more, the two families were like one in many ways. When Al Rumely decided to run for mayor, my father and mother were two of his strongest political support-ers. When Al won the race, my parents threw a huge celebra-tion dinner for them.

Mother had always said we came and went out of each others' houses so much that she got schedules out of whack one time too many.

When something bizarre and of cataclysmic magnitude occurs to someone you love, the shock is more than debilitat-ing; it sends a grief so piercing that sometimes the only way to deal with it and survive is to deny.

The night my mother got the phone call that both Al and Fran had been shot multiple times while lying asleep in their bed by a crazed ex–city employee, who blamed the mayor for the loss of his job at the city sanitation department, my mother didn't believe it. Fran was like her sister, really, *more* than her sister. Fran was, well, irreplaceable.

Fran's death left a hole inside the Lanigan family that nothing or no one could ever fill.

Fran had died instantly. Incredibly, Al had not.

For weeks, Al clung to life by the use of every stitch of modern medical technology available at the time. I remember the anger that assaulted all the Rumely children, now all adults, like a riptide of unparalleled force.

Finally, unable to battle the impossible, Al, too, succumbed to death.

"Dad didn't choose this way to die!" one of the girls had said to me. "This isn't fair. Isn't fair!"

Both funerals left me numb. To lose Fran and Al was like losing my own parents. Sometimes I believed that half the wonderful dictums, say-sos and teachings I received in my childhood were straight from Fran's lips. Now she was gone.

As painful as it was for me and my siblings, Fran's death sent my mother spiraling into sadness. I can remember her picking up the phone and dialing Fran's number and then putting it down. "I forgot. She's not there."

Or when something funny would happen or Mother would hear a special joke, she would say, "I have to remember that joke to tell Fran. . . ." Then Mother's voice would trail off, I'd see a tear and know how much she missed her best friend.

It is so interesting to me about how the departed come to visit us. I know that Fran sensed Mother's pain. But no matter what I would say to Mother to comfort her, the void was there.

One night only a month or so after Fran died, Nancy had one of the most real dreams of her life.

In the dream Nancy heard the telephone ring. She picked up the phone and answered it.

"Hello?" Nancy said.

"Nan. This is Fran. Listen, do me a favor, sweetness. Tell your mother not to worry about me. I'm just fine."

"Fran, is that you?"

"Yes, dear. It's me. Tell her that I would have called her sooner, but they just have me so busy over here."

"They?"

"Yes. It's amazing here."

"And where is here?"

"Why, heaven, of course, dear."

"I don't understand, Fran," Nancy said. "How could you be busy in heaven? What are you doing?"

"Why, I'm giving needlepoint classes one right after the other. I barely have time to breathe."

"Needlepoint."

"Sure. Still doing my own designs. Look, tell your mother. I have to run."

Before Nancy could ask any more questions, Fran had hung up without saying good-bye.

Nancy awoke instantly from the dream and called Mother and me to tell us about the dream.

"It was really Fran, Mother. I swear it was. You know how she always just hangs up and forgets to say good-bye!"

"I know, Nan," Mother said. "I've corrected her about that for years. But it's also our sign that she really is in heaven doing just as she says she is."

"You think they really have needlepoint classes in heaven?" I asked.

Mother paused. "Well, why not? No one is as gifted as Fran with a needle. And her designs were positively heavenly. It would make Fran happy to stay busy like that and share her vision with others. Sure, I believe it."

The peaceful sound of acceptance in Mother's voice told Nancy and me what we needed to know. Mother was finally at ease with Fran's passing. She had wanted a sign from Fran, and now she had one.

In the decades since then, not once have either Mother or I doubted for a minute that Fran telephoned Nancy from heaven that night. Fran had always loved Mother, and Mother loved her in return. It would have been just like Fran to want to call Mother . . . just to say "hello." All the way from heaven.

Angel of Death, Thou Art Banished!

Houston, Texas. 1973.

ndrew Shiro was only seven months old when he faced his second encounter with death (see "The Medical Team from the Other Side"). Though the ileostomy performed on infant Andrew within the first weeks of his birth had saved his life, it wasn't long before the small intestine had begun to act like his diseased large intestine.

Vicki and Andy rushed their son to Texas Children's Hospital and discovered that Dr. Harberg, who had performed the first surgery, was out of the country and would not return from Germany for weeks.

The staff doctors told Vicki that Andrew's intestine was now retaining his stool, and that it was too large to pass through the hole in his flesh into the tube. Because the disease was rare, and because Dr. Harberg was a specialist dealing with a new procedure, the doctors did not know how to treat Andrew.

In a matter of days, despite all of Vicki's exacting attention to his diet and care, Andrew had lost eight pounds and was dehydrated.

He hovered close to death.

The hospital found Dr. Harberg in Germany. He didn't trust anyone with Andrew's life. He booked a flight back to Houston. "You just keep that baby alive until I get there," he ordered.

All Vicki could do was pray.

Andrew was admitted into the hospital, and the staff provided Vicki with a cot in his room since she was determined not to leave his side.

Because of the dehydration, the doctor needed to insert an IV to save Andrew's life. However, his veins were rolling and they could not find a good vein. Never having any medical training at all, Vicki was not privy to procedures or medical slang. The dilemma of watching Andrew fighting for his life, and not being able to insert an IV, nearly drove Vicki crazy.

Suddenly, from either inside her head or one of the voices from the spiritual medical team from the Other Side, she heard, "Tell them to do a cut down."

Vicki looked at the nurse and the doctor. "Do a cut down."

"What?"

"Do you know what a cut down is?" Vicki asked.

"We do. But do you?"

"Yes," Vicki replied staunchly. Then she repeated out loud what she was being told from her angels. "You will cut the vein open, insert the IV needle and then suture up the skin."

"What kind of training do you have, Mrs. Shiro?" the doctor asked.

"I know enough to realize that this is what we have to do!

Now are you going to do it? Or should I just do it myself? I will, you know!"

"Okay. Okay," the nurse said.

Vicki looked at Andrew. He was slipping away before her eyes.

"He's my only child. I'll hold him down while you do it."

"Very well," the doctor replied and sent the nurse for the instruments.

In minutes, the cut was made, the IV needle properly inserted in Andrew's vein and sutures correctly made.

The IV liquid seeped into Andrew. Only time would tell if he would make it.

Or so Vicki thought.

That night a storm raged. As Andrew dozed and then slept, Vicki kept her prayer vigil going. Thunder rolled and lightning split the sky as each prayer rolled off her lips. There were times when she wondered if she was being defied or encouraged by the power of the storm outside.

"Give me strength to make it through this. Give me enough strength to fight one more hour. Help me, God. Please help me. Let Andrew live."

In the darkened room, only the night-light under the vanity glowed. Sitting on the cot, her head resting on Andrew's crib, she stared at the night-light and prayed.

Like something out of a demonic thriller movie, Vicki distinctly saw black billowing smoke rise from the floor. At first she thought there was a fire.

She opened her mouth to warn the nurses about the fire and realized this wasn't ordinary smoke.

Rising in eight distinct shapes, the smoke forms circled Andrew's bed and hovered there.

Vicki sat upright.

"I know who you are!" she shouted. "You are the Angels of Death. You cannot come for my son! I won't let you have him!"

Bolting off the cot, Vicki threw her body directly over Andrew. "You can't take him. I'm the mother! Go away. Go back to hell where you came from! Go there alone! You cannot have my son, now or anytime while I am alive!"

Tears seared Vicki's cheeks, but her determination and defiance forced the Angels to retreat from the crib.

They moved away from the bed to the end of the room where they seemed to melt away, then slip into the cracks in the floor.

"That's right! Go back to hell!" she shouted at them as she climbed off the bed. Keeping her right hand over Andrew's heart, she infused him with all her courage and love.

For the rest of the night she did not sleep but stood sentry over Andrew, her hand on his heart, his life in her hand.

When morning came, Andrew had turned a corner. Color washed his cheeks. Dr. Harberg phoned in that he'd landed at the airport and was on his way to the hospital. Andrew was prepped for another surgery. Vicki said a prayer of thanksgiving.

Two days later Andrew was cooing in Vicki's arms as they drove back home once again. This time, Vicki had learned about more than a medical procedure or the marvels of contemporary medicine.

She learned that nothing on this earth is stronger than a mother's prayer.

Heaven Will Find Me

I love music, all kinds of music. However, in our family when it came to handing out the musical talent, I got passed over. Oh, I sang in the parochial school choir until eighth grade when life pushes you out of the nest into high school where you are told, "Music isn't your bag." The only instrument I ever learned to play was a radio. I could fine-tune that dial on a Saturday night and pick up Nashville, Tennessee, or Detroit, and sometimes a disc jockey in New Jersey would come through. When my parents invested in a high-fidelity console player, I would play 78s and sing along at the top of my lungs. I played to an empty room.

My musical talent has strictly been in the appreciation mode.

I explain all this so that you can understand how far-fetched my desire to write a song has been. I came to the awareness about twenty years ago that someday I would write a song. I was in a marriage counselor's office, and he was conducting an experiment to judge whether I was stable or not, I assume. He asked me to close my eyes and envision a quiet place.

I chose a beautiful wooded scene with a lovely path. On this path, I was to "see" someone who came to my aid. In my vision, I saw my friend Cherry. She came up to me and lovingly put her arm around me, and we walked down the path together. Then the counselor said, "Others will join you on the path. Who are they?"

At that point my vision took on the most interesting course. I saw cartoon caricatures of the Oscar, the Emmy and the Grammy. When you think about it, they are the names of people: Oscar, Emily and Grandmother.

When I opened my eyes and explained to the counselor what I saw, he asked, "What do they symbolize to you?"

"Why, they are tokens of my esteem," I smiled.

The counselor told me not to come back. I didn't need him, he said. I couldn't have agreed more.

Since that time, the idea of writing a song has flitted across my mind like an illusionary butterfly. It's a beautiful idea, but hardly practical. I had other things to write, and besides, I'd never even written poetry, much less something someone would want to put music to. Besides, doesn't one need to go to school to learn that kind of thing?

Over the years I have had the privilege of meeting music producers and performers. I've sat in on jam sessions, been at a Los Angeles music production studio all night and watched in awe as "real" songwriters created magic with "real" musicians and "real" composers. Still, the world of music was Greek to me. I could appreciate it, but I never thought I could do it.

During the past several years I have been working on a particular film project for teens and kids. It's called *The Adventures of Lillie and Zane: The Secret of the Seven Stones*. I created the original character of Lillie Mitchell ten years ago, so she's been in my mind and heart for quite some time. Once I started working on this new adventure for Lillie, the idea of writing a song just for her began to gel in my mind. I felt the desire to write a song for her, but not a single word ever manifested either in my brain or on paper.

One night, I bolted awake at about five in the morning. A booming, demanding, commanding male voice said, "Cathy, wake up!"

It was a voice I hadn't heard in many, many years. It was the voice that only came to me when my life was in danger or I was about to turn some incredible corner in my life. It was Mr. Voice.

Mr. Voice is the name I have given to my most powerful guardian angel. This angel doesn't mess around. When he shows up, I listen. It isn't a voice inside me. It's not something or someone who speaks up on a daily, monthly or even yearly basis. Mr. Voice's appearances are rare, indeed.

When he told me to wake up, I did!

"What?" I said, my eyes wide open.

"Wake up!"

"I'm awake," I replied holding my breath, squinting through the darkness. Suddenly, I realized it was indeed Mr. Voice. My first thought was that he was here to tell me that Mother had died. Or Nan had crashed on the airplane. It was always something dire when Mr. Voice showed up. I didn't like any of this. First of all, few people in my life anymore call me "Cathy," except for my very immediate family. It's either Catherine or Cath. This was another confirmation that my guardian angel had shown up and not some false spirit pretending to be Mr. Voice.

I felt perspiration sprout all over my face. I gripped the sheets and held my breath waiting for instruction.

"Write the song," he said.

"What song?"

"Go upstairs now! Do not go back to sleep. Write the song."

"I . . . I don't have a song. I know of no song. . . ."

"Do it!"

I jumped out of the bed so fast one would have thought the thing had caught on fire. I didn't dare lie back down. I flew up the stairs to my study and turned on the computer. I had no clue what I would write, what it was supposed to say, the story it would tell or even how the song would end. There was not a single note in my head.

I put my hands on the keys, and they clacked away.

Shocked, I watched as the cursor moved across my screen and left this trail of fabulous, visual, melancholy words that told a story of true love. In a single poem, Mr. Voice created the germ, the inner soul of Lillie's story.

I lost track of time. In less than twenty minutes the initial song was down in black-and-white pixels, though not on paper. Over the next hour I tinkered with the words, making them move a bit better, rhyme a little more.

When I finished, I printed it out and read it. It brought tears to my eyes. I thanked Mr. Voice for allowing his song to come through me.

One thing needs to be stated very clearly: I didn't write this song. It came through me. It was given to me. A great big celestial, angelic gift for me to give to the world and to whoever will hear it.

I called my friend Wendy and told her about the song. She

said, "Cath, let me read it." So I faxed a copy to her.

In seconds she phoned me back. "I have goose bumps! This song is going to be great!"

"It's not really a song, you know. It's just a poem. That's all," I said.

"No, it's not!" Wendy insisted. "It's going to be a real song. I could sing it for you!"

"You will?"

"Sure! I have a feeling about this song. You're the one who is always telling us to pay attention to our intuitions. Well, I'm listening with all ears!"

Later that day I went to Ron for my scheduled massage. While working the knots out of my hands, I told Ron about Mr. Voice and the song he'd given me that morning.

"Who is going to write the music?" Ron asked.

"I don't know. I haven't even thought about it. I'm still so stunned that I actually helped bring this pretty poem to life."

"Why not let me give it a try?" Ron said.

Now I'd vaguely remembered that Ron had given me a tape of a New Age–type composition he'd written many years ago, but it was not a thought on my front burner. As often happens with me, I smacked my forehead and said, "Duh, why didn't I think of that?"

"Dense?" he teased.

Later that day, I phoned Ron and read the words to him off the computer. Then I went back to working on a screenplay that needed more help than even Mr. Voice could provide, I'm afraid.

Two days later, Ron called to tell me that he, too, had nearly the same experience.

"I have the music for your song. It was the strangest thing. It just flowed, and I haven't written any music in years! You have to hear this. I think it's very special."

A week later I did have a chance to hear the music, and it was inspiring and uplifting. By this time, I'd taken Wendy up on her offer to sing. All three of us got together with guitarist, Joe, a friend of Wendy's, and taped the first rendition of the song. The bridge needed work. I rewrote a line. I added two lines. But that was all. The rest of the song remained just as Mr. Voice had written it.

Several weeks later, Ron had gone home to New York, and when he returned, he called to say he'd reworked the bridge music. The words stayed the same, but the music was better. Wendy joined us a week later, and we taped another session.

What has been so interesting to all of us is the magic of our own creativities blending to make a single statement. We are by no means finished with the process required to get the song produced and sold, but we are nearly there. Most people would warn us that the chances of our song ever being played on a radio or used in a movie are slim to none, but we don't care. What is most important to me is that my friends believe in me and my Mr. Voice enough to want to continue on this difficult, time-consuming, possibly heartbreaking, yet creatively rewarding path we have chosen. No one may ever like our song as much as we do. We may never get it produced and out to the public, and we may not succeed at using it for the base of a score for a film, but for the rest of our lives we know one thing—we believed and we took a chance. The rest is up to God.

Near-Death
Experiences

READER/CUSTOMER CARE SURVEY

We care about your opinions! Please take a moment to fill out our online Reader Survey at **http://survey.hcibooks.com**.

As a **"THANK YOU"** you will receive a **VALUABLE INSTANT COUPON** towards future book purchases as well as a **SPECIAL GIFT** available only online! Or, you may mail this card back to us and we will send you a copy of our exciting catalog with your valuable coupon inside.

(PLEASE PRINT IN ALL CAPS)

First Name _____ MI. _____ Last Name _____

Address _____

State _____ Zip _____ City _____ Email _____

1. Gender
❑ Female ❑ Male

2. Age
❑ 8 or younger
❑ 9-12   ❑ 13-16
❑ 17-20   ❑ 21-30
❑ 31+

3. Did you receive this book as a gift?
❑ Yes ❑ No

4. Annual Household Income
❑ under $25,000
❑ $25,000 - $34,999
❑ $35,000 - $49,999
❑ $50,000 - $74,999
❑ over $75,000

5. What are the ages of the children living in your house?
❑ 0 - 14 ❑ 15+

6. Marital Status
❑ Single
❑ Married
❑ Divorced
❑ Widowed

7. How did you find out about the book?
(please choose one)
❑ Recommendation
❑ Store Display
❑ Online
❑ Catalog/Mailing
❑ Interview/Review

8. Where do you usually buy books?
(please choose one)
❑ Bookstore
❑ Online
❑ Book Club/Mail Order
❑ Price Club (Sam's Club, Costco's, etc.)
❑ Retail Store (Target, Wal-Mart, etc.)

9. What subject do you enjoy reading about the most?
(please choose one)
❑ Parenting/Family
❑ Relationships
❑ Recovery/Addictions
❑ Health/Nutrition
❑ Christianity
❑ Spirituality/Inspiration
❑ Business Self-help
❑ Women's Issues
❑ Sports

10. What attracts you most to a book?
(please choose one)
❑ Title
❑ Cover Design
❑ Author
❑ Content

TAPE IN MIDDLE; DO NOT STAPLE

BUSINESS REPLY MAIL

FIRST-CLASS MAIL PERMIT NO 45 DEERFIELD BEACH, FL

POSTAGE WILL BE PAID BY ADDRESSEE

Health Communications, Inc.
3201 SW 15th Street
Deerfield Beach FL 33442-9875

FOLD HERE

Comments

imply put, "near-death experiences" or NDEs, as they are called, are those instances in which a person actually "dies" clinically, or comes extremely close to death so as to think one has died at least momentarily, and that person experiences some kind of spiritual encounter or event during those moments of death and then returns to life. In nearly all cases, the perspective/paradigm of the person going through the experience is altered drastically.

Christians sometimes call these events a "St. Paul Conversion." Often after these events, there are people who experience a drastic personality alteration. For example, a bully who has an NDE may realize the error of his ways and change his attitude 180 degrees.

I make a joke about it, but I have said far too often in life when meeting an egotistical, uncaring and clueless human being, "There's nothing wrong with that person that a really good near-death experience wouldn't cure."

Of all the angelic encounters that exist, this one is the big kahuna. Nobody dies, sees heaven and returns to earth without suddenly understanding what LIFE is all about. Once you've had this experience and live to tell about it, you can rest assured the next time around you probably won't be coming back.

Life is not a dress rehearsal.

You better get it right.

Because I didn't want this book to be just about near-death experiences, I have limited these experiences to just two, mine and that of Judy Fry. This is my second near-death experience and has not been told until now. I have endeavored not to leave anything out. This was the most difficult story for me to tell because there *was* so much to tell.

If this kind of information is of particular interest to you, you should know that there are dozens of books on the market over the past twenty years about near-death experiences. Dannion Brinkley's book *Saved by the Light* was one of the first, along with those by Melvin Morse. Consult the bibliography at the back of this book for more titles on the subject.

Death Becomes an Angel

All my life I have accepted the fact that there is an afterlife. My formal education, life experiences and further research has revealed to me that there is a before life as well.

Just yesterday I was speaking with a friend who confided in me that she was not certain as to whether she believed in life after death or not. She was "vacillating" she told me. She had watched a recent television program about a psychic who sees dead people and can solve murder mysteries. She wasn't sure she believed this was real. Wasn't this just a story line dreamed up by some writers to sell a television program?

At that moment, I was reminded that there are others who are not sure about this life and the one after. My first *Angel Watch* book and this book as well have been written with the assumptions that the reader understands there *is* an afterlife, and that the reader wants more information about what it is like.

Perhaps if you, the reader, are like my dear friend, you are searching for answers in your life, and I can only pray that the information I am about to give you here will help in some small measure to guide you. I do not believe it is within my power to give absolutes of any kind. I am not a theologian. However, as in most near-death experiences, the life of the "experiencer" is vastly altered after the encounter with the divine.

We are all part of God. We are God's thoughts. God created us, and I believe that we all have God in us. That is why we are all connected to each other and are part of each others' lives. Of all the creations that man has conjured, that of war is the most insidious to our well-being. Would I want to cut off my own leg or cut out my own heart? Why then, would I want to kill another living being? It's bad enough that our ecological system is set up to devour fish, fowl, beast and plants in order to survive. This system of creation, I believe, is based upon "unconditional love" of the plants and beasts giving their energy to us to create an even better world. But are we doing that?

It is important for us to give thanks to the earth and animals for the food they offer us. It is important for us to thank God by our daily actions toward one another by offering kindness rather than hatred or bitterness to each other.

We are all part of the One.

It is my hope that this story of my near-death experience will not only illustrate the life after death but illuminate as well.

No amount of talent, skill or insight can describe what I am about to relate in the following encounter, just as no poet or song can accurately define "love." It is part of the human condition to be limited in all things. The limitations and liabilities of language hinder my ability to bring heaven to these pages. This is simply a mortal's attempt at the divine. Even in the attempt, I will fail.

I'll never know on this side of the Veil if I truly died the night of my last surgery, but I believe that I did.

My "death" was not recorded on a monitor. To my knowledge the doctors did not "lose" me like they did the morning my son was born. However, the night before the operation I called my son, Ryan, into my study to talk to him for what I believed would be the last time.

I had an overwhelming sensation that I would not come out of this surgery alive. Though my doctor had told me that the tumor on my ovary was the size of a four-month-old fetus, we did not know if this time there was cancer like I'd had six years earlier. Given my track record, it didn't look good.

I've had a handful of major surgeries in my life. I'm not doing any more of them, I can tell you. At least I sure pray not! Despite all that, I had never before called my mother and requested that she come to be with me during my surgery or my recovery. This time, however, I told her that I needed her with me because I did not think I would live through it. Mother got on a plane and flew to Houston from Indiana within hours of my call.

I sat with Ryan, who was then in college but still living at home during the summer with us.

I told Ryan where I'd put what little jewelry I had and that I wanted him to save it for my granddaughter someday.

"How do you know it's a girl?"

"I just know that you will have a daughter. I don't know how many children you will have, but at least one will be a girl," I assured him. For many people, women's intuition is not "knowing" something for certain, nor does it make that knowing a fact. In our household, my son knew me well enough to know that there are just some things Mom does know. All that aside, I figured odds were that God would let me have a granddaughter since I didn't get a daughter of my own, and I would have loved that. It was a hope.

I told him where I'd stashed some money for his graduation, where to find my will, the keys to my lockbox and a list of items I wanted my sister and mother to have.

Ryan had tears in his eyes. "I can't believe you're saying all this, Mom. What's the matter? Don't you want to live? Don't you want to fight this?"

"It's not like that, Ryan," I said. "It's this incredibly strong feeling I have that everything will be so vastly different after this surgery."

"How?"

I looked around the room. I could see it recede from me as if it were being sucked down a long tunnel. "I won't be living in this house."

"That's ridiculous," Ryan replied.

"Nothing will be the same. Your stepfather is going to ask me for a divorce."

"No way," Ryan said.

I avoided his eyes. Even as I spoke the words I knew the callous truth of my situation in life at that point. "I don't want to be buried here in Houston. Mother knows this. I told her I want to be buried next to my twin sisters in the family plot, if that's possible."

"Mom, this is too creepy. If you talk like this, you can make it happen."

"I'm being practical."

"Mom, I don't want you to leave. You're the only mom I've got. I need you! You have to stay here for me."

We hugged for the longest time and cried even longer. I remembered too well the morning Ryan was born and that I had nearly died. I was so young then, only twenty-four. When the angel asked me if I wanted to go back to earth and live for my son, I "chose" to come back for Ryan. I loved him more than anything on the day of his birth, when I didn't even know him. Now that he was grown, I cherished his every breath. He was the best part of me, the best human being I had ever known. I knew I should have been trying to reassure him that I would never leave him. I should have been making all kinds of hope-filled promises.

My emotions didn't make any sense to me. I could not understand why I was feeling this impending finiteness. Oddly, I was incredibly resigned to what I believed would be my death.

"I'll try to stay, Ryan, but if it's God's will I leave, I have to go. I'll still love you. I'll still be right by your side, just like Ethan, your brother, is always with us. If you look for me, you can find me. You will feel my presence with you. I know I can make that happen for us."

"Mom, let's be practical. You can't bake me cookies from heaven."

I smiled and wiped his tears with my fingers. "I'll remember that."

The following morning, going to the hospital and the pre-op prep were procedures I knew too well. Mother had flown in the night before and stayed at our house. My soon-to-be ex-husband went through the motions of courtesy, but that was all.

Frankly, I was surprised he even went to the hospital with us.

I hugged my mother for what I thought was the last time, and then they wheeled me down the hall to the operating room.

The anesthesiologist plunged me into blackness.

The black sea buoyed me up, allowing me to float until I came to stand on a rock in the middle of the sea.

Suddenly, the space around me opened as if there were a rift in the sky. I had no sense of time, so I don't know how far into the surgery I was. In my experience, there was no sense of time and no real sense of place. There was only space, universes around me, and I felt a part of all of it. I was a mere speck and was struck at how insignificant I was; and yet, I saw my own light shining from within me, shooting outward as if I was the brightest star in the sky or in this space.

An enormous angel appeared, nearly twenty-five to thirty feet tall. His wingspan was another thirty to forty feet.

I was shocked that I didn't fall to my knees, but I did not.

"Who are you?" I asked.

"I am here to give you strength, for you have none."

"That's true. I have none." I was very surprised that this angel would know exactly what I needed at this point in my life, even when I had been unable to admit it to myself. These simple words filled me with courage and overwhelming hope. Even when we don't feel brave or strong, just to have *hope* gives us the will to go on living and to keep trying to do better every day. I realized that, for quite some time, I had been running out of hope.

"Touch my wing," he commanded.

To this day I am impressed with this angel's voice. I had expected his voice to boom, like Mr. Voice's, whom I believe is my guardian angel, but it did not. In fact, it had a timbre to it that was at once melodious and ringing. There was strength in his voice and incredible love. I felt resoundingly loved all at once. His voice resonated through my body somewhat like music does when it's turned up very loud. But this was more than that. It was as if these echoes were filtering through my skin into my cellular structure and tuning them, healing them or making something new that had previously been old. I had the sensation that something was happening internally to me as he spoke.

This was not a conscious processing of information at that time. It was like a blast of knowledge of what was going on that I simply accepted. I remember thinking that I suddenly had *all* the answers, that I knew things about the workings of the universe, about God, and about how to access my Source through my heart, mind and soul in a way I had never thought before. Suddenly, all of life seemed easy. Simple. Logical.

"Touch my wing," he said again.

"I can't touch your wing."

"Touch it," he said, still using that gentle command.

"I'm afraid."

"I know that. Be brave."

Suddenly, I was filled with confidence and courage; more than I had known in my entire life. I nearly felt superhuman. I moved over and raised my hand to the wing to my right, which was his left wing.

I say here, "his," but I don't mean that I thought this angel was a man. Though his size brought my human mind to process his "beingness" as more masculine in gender, this was not the case. His protectiveness and nurturing qualities were feminine or maternal in nature. My best claim is to say that I believed the angel to be androgynous.

He wore long white robes, gowns. The fabric was diaphanous, glittering with a white that shone in all manner of colors of the rainbow, but when blended, I would call them "diamond light."

This aspect is quite important, I believe. Diamond light is a protective "armor" of sorts that I believe we can all envision around ourselves, our bodies, houses and families to protect them from negative forces/thoughts/vibrations. This diamond light is not the same as silver light or golden light. As I viewed it while standing there next to this thirty-foot angel, it reminded me of Michael the archangel's battle gear, worn when he fights Lucifer. I thought of that phrase, "hard as a diamond."

On earth it is true there is no harder substance than a diamond. Is it possible the reason humans value diamonds so highly is because our souls know that diamond light is impenetrable? Over the years when I have felt that I was up against something or someone whose intentions I was convinced were not honorable, I would envision myself surrounded in a bubble of diamond light. Interestingly, most of these folks left my life or my presence rather quickly. The phrase "the dark cannot live in the light" has been proven to me numerous times.

Looking up at the angel, I gathered my courage and touched the wing. As I write this, I can still feel every sensation of that encounter.

The bone of the wing was like a steel girder and just as wide. It was approximately twelve inches across the flat top of the bone before falling down into the flesh and smaller bones that made up the wing. I pressed my hand against the flesh. It was quite soft and very warm. I could feel the pulse of this incredible animal, and yes, I thought the word "animal." It had a heart, blood, muscle, bone and skin. And it had feathers.

I have never spoken about the feathers or the placement of those feathers to anyone before this date, and today I know the reason why.

I was recently on a local television program, *The Debra Duncan Show,* in which three sisters related their encounter when their mother passed from the earth plane through the tunnel to the Other Side. One of the women actually saw their mother's soul rise out of her body, turn into a glowing white light, become a young woman again and then sprout wings.

Fantastic as it sounds, I frankly didn't believe her. Here I was, an author of a book about angels, and I did not believe what I was hearing only because I'd never come across this kind of revelation in any research I had conducted. I was taught to believe, and my research revealed, that humans were humans and angels were angels. This kind of evolution of spirit was a new take for me. Could this be true that humans have now reached a new phase of their spiritual evolution?

The woman proceeded to describe the angel's wings her mother had. It was then I realized I had been waiting for my own validation of my near-death experience from a decade earlier. Her mother's angel wings were exactly the same as the angel I experienced in my near-death experience. Now that I've received this information, I am prepared to share my total experience.

My angel's wing was covered in white feathers. They were bird feathers. These were not made of light or color or some see-through wimpy fabric. These were real honest-to-goodness feathers.

Snowy white, yes. Glowing? No. They were layered over one another in a symmetrical pattern that left little flesh between the pores where the feathers grew. At first touch, I thought the angel's flesh was rough, but then I realized it was because there were so many feathers, there was little room for anything else.

This angel was as real as the chickens on my grandfather's ranch.

This was my shock.

"Get on my back," the angel said.

Shock number two.

"We're going somewhere?"

"You need to see why my wings are so big. So strong."

"How did you know what I was thinking?" The minute I said it, I thought, "That was dumb. Angels know everything."

"I don't know everything. Only God knows everything," it said, reading my thoughts.

The angel put his palm down, and I climbed into it, feeling a bit like Faye Wray with King Kong. It put me on its back at the apex where the neck meets the shoulders.

The angel had blond hair. I held the hair like it was a set of reins.

"Are you ready?"

"I am," I said.

"Hold very tight. I will not drop you, but you must do your part."

Like in one of those sci-fi movies, we shot through the night sky at warp speed. I would have liked the sensation of rising above the earth and seeing the planet fade in the distance like the astronauts do, but no. We zoomed. The universes zipping past us were so numerous they began to blend into a myriad of white lines that eventually did look like a tunnel, I suppose.

Perhaps this is the tunnel of light that other NDE people describe in their experiences. However, when we finally landed, halted, stopped or whatever, it was green.

I remembered my mother saying that when her Aunt Violet was dying she kept saying over and over, "It's so green, Dorothy. Paradise is green."

It was green. And yellow. And pink. And blue.

It was a landscape like none I have ever seen, though it was similar to earth.

The sky was blue but with shots of gold and orange and red as if the sun were constantly setting and rising or both simultaneously.

The grass was an illuminated green. Here, it did look like there were "up lights" on every blade of grass. The flowers appeared to be lit from within or had lightbulbs inside to make them glisten. I suppose if the place had been made of ice, and the ice was colored, that would explain it. Or if it was made of gemstones. But the grass was soft. Softer than velvet. It was like silk or cashmere and was the softest thing you can imagine.

I was struck with the realization that there was no dirt. Everything was immaculate. Even here my humor surfaced, and I thought, "They must vacuum all the time here!"

The trees were impeccably trimmed, much like boxwoods and holly in those formal French and English gardens of the late 1700s.

I stood on a grassy hill with a river flowing from east to west below me. The angel took me to the river's edge. I looked down into the river and saw my reflection. However, the water was not transparent, as you would expect. It had a mirror effect. I realized the river was mercury. (I have spoken in confidence to several other people who have had near-death experiences, and this "mercury" river is one of their "tests" to see if the person they are comparing notes with actually died and experienced the same thing or not.)

"I'll fly you over," the angel said.

"Don't I have to walk through?" In my mind I thought I would have to "wash my sins."

"There are no sins here."

He motioned with his arm to his left. In a space that looked like a hole in the sky because it was dark, I saw a series of "bubbles." I now have heard others refer to this black hole in the sky that I saw as a "movie screen" on which the viewer was able to see all his past lives in an instant. This is the "past-life review" or "life review" many NDE experiencers mention.

In each of these bubbles were times when I had lived, or was in the process of living (if you believe there is no such thing as time and that all events are occurring simultaneously). It is important to note that the bubbles were pink in color (if one needed to ascribe a color to them). They were transparent, however. Each bubble would take volumes to describe each life, which I do not have the time to relate here. However, these hundreds or more lives "passed" in what seemed like a millisecond. Then it was over.

In a single flash I reexperienced all my pains, sorrows, joys and love. There was no judgment from the angel or anyone else. It is also important to note that the "pain" I experienced was not the pain that I had suffered, *but was the pain, usually emotional pain, that I had caused others.* This aspect of the review is incredibly important. Though many of us in our ego-centeredness believe that what we have endured through our lives is painful, it is not an iota of the agony you will endure due to the anger, intolerance and spitefulness you have inflicted on another in this life. Their pain at your hands will be visited on you during this review. Therefore, it would be wise to remember this fact each time you feel the urge to lash out at those you believe are not doing right by you. Consider their feelings first. Remember that once you speak those discouraging words to another person, you can never take them back and they are etched on the ethers of eternity. Those words and actions are *yours.* Good or bad. It's always *your* choice.

When asking others about their near-death experiences or a life review, I can spot the charlatans from a mile away because they fail to mention this all-important incident and primary aspect of the past-life review.

We are here on earth to learn the lesson of love; of giving love to others. If we don't learn our lesson and give unconditionally of ourselves, we keep coming back again and again. Criminals and diabolical murderers will face the "pain" they inflicted on others. They will suffer as they made others suffer. I believe this is what "karma" is all about. I don't believe in hell, per se, but on the other hand, knowing what that life review was like and how horrid it could be if I had led a life of meanness and evil would be hell enough.

I saw the scenes of the life I was living all at once. It was as if I was born, lived and died all in an instant. I was struck by the fact that no one judged me. I was to judge myself. I was both filled with emotion and yet objective at the same time. In many ways it was as if I were someone else.

Interestingly, I saw myself in-between lives here in this *heaven.* I saw myself coming up to heaven several times and making the decision not to die or leave yet, which even now seems odd, but factual.

In my current life, I was pleased that I had been sent to earth to love and had indeed loved those I "owed" a lifetime to. This "owing" them stemmed from previous lives when I had not loved as well as I should have. Each time I had held back my love, I judged myself as lacking. I was "disappointed" with myself in those lives.

To this day, these "bubble scenes" are one of my hidden validations to know if someone is telling me the truth when they say they died and came back. Also, the bubbles are not hard, but like liquid pink light with many colors revolving around the edge or wall of the bubble. When you touch it, it moves like moving a liquid, and it is lukewarm, not hot or cold to the touch. I have also now known gifted people who have accessed these bubbles in very deep meditation or prayer, but this is rare.

In the next instant I was on the angel's back, across the river and off its back, and the angel vanished. I stood on a golden-bricked path. I don't know if this was from too many viewings of the movie *Wizard of Oz* or not, but indeed the road was golden light. The area here was very manicured. The trees again were as if they had been shaped and pruned to perfection. The flowers were spectacular. I saw a lot of roses and could smell rose scent. There were lilies, orchids, pansies, daisies and very bizarre flowers that must exist on parts of the earth I have not seen, or perhaps on another planet. The air was thin and clean. The clouds were brilliant snowy white in an azure sky, and I remember seeing more than one moon. The silver or mercury river was just behind me but curved to the left of me.

When I turned around after looking for the angel, I came face-to-face with a man whom I perceived to be Jesus. He was tall and thin with a medium build. He had strawberry blond hair that touched his shoulders. I could not actually look upon his face, as the light emanating from him was so intense, it hurt to look at him. I had the impression, though honestly I did not actually see, that he had a reddish-blond beard cut short with a mustache. I remembered in my mind's eye that the shape of his face was long and quite angular. I remember having the impression his eyes were blue-gray or gray, but the truth was that his eyes were silver. They were perfect light. Again, the "silver eyes of Jesus" is another clue I use when speaking to others who have said they have encountered Jesus in a dream, meditation or near-death experience to validate if that other person is telling the truth.

It is interesting to note that since the time of this near-death experience, there have been many archaeological discoveries that should be addressed.

Archaeologists have discovered that the famed "Shroud of Turin" is not the cloth that covered Christ, but carbon dating and other newer forms of dating prove that the shroud cannot predate the year 1240.

These scholars believe the shroud is the one used to bury Jacques de Molay, the last Grand Master of the Knights Templars who fought valiantly in the Crusades. However, Jacques was tortured for his beliefs by King Philip of France, or "Philip the Fair," and Pope Clement in 1307. Jacques was labeled a heretic, and Philip the Fair seized the treasury of the Templars, which included the largest group of landed gentry in all of Christendom.

When he was sentenced to death Jacques requested to be crucified in exactly the same manner as Jesus. He was then crowned with thorns, flogged, crucified and his side was lanced. Therefore, all the body markings of Christ were evident in the shroud, which is why for so many centuries Christians have believed the shroud to be Jesus's shroud.

Jacques de Molay was over six feet tall with a slender build and a long angular face with shoulder-length hair.

It is from the Shroud of Turin that most medieval painters, and later most artists of the Western world, drew their concept of what Jesus looked like. In my upbringing I have only seen Jesus depicted in this manner.

Since that time, historians in search of the historical Christ have indeed proven that he did live, and is in fact a historical figure, just as the New Testament portrays. (This has been in question for those not of the Christian faith.) From passages in the New Testament, the Dead Sea Scrolls and the Gnostic Gospels, some historians have recently (2002) claimed that Jesus of Nazareth was short, dark-haired, dark-skinned (as were most Jewish people in that area at that time), and possibly had a hunchback. Remember that all this information is the "newest archaeological theory." There is no doubt in my mind that next year, another archaeological team or Dead Sea Scroll transcriber will come up with another theory still.

I do not know for certain if the man I saw in my encounter was truly Jesus. Perhaps he was Jacques de Molay, which would make this man a saint, having been falsely accused of crimes trumped up by Philip the Fair who only wanted the Templars' money and land.

Perhaps the man I met was an angel or a "light being," a messenger of sorts. He never said he was Jesus. He never gave me any name, but then, I didn't ask. I assumed he was Jesus.

The force of the love emanating from him was so powerful, so profound, and so utterly unconditional that it sent me to my knees, crying at the wonder of it. I was incredibly humbled; more than I have ever felt or even knew was possible. I felt completely and totally loved for myself and myself alone. It was an emotion I have never felt on the earth plane. The intensity of it is just indescribable.

"My Lord and my Master," I said through racking sobs. I was awed to be in his presence, and I can remember thinking, "Surely Jesus has a lot of important things he should be doing. What is he doing talking to me?" Still, his indescribable love kept flooding me.

"You're not done yet," he said.

A thousand thoughts went through me. They were not just my thoughts, but Universal Knowledge of a magnitude that should have been overwhelming, but was not. Suddenly, I was at peace with everything in my life, with life itself, and so full of love that nothing mattered except being in this place and being with Jesus. I said nothing but raised my head.

I still could not look directly at him. Therefore, I glanced off to his right, my left. In the distance I saw what looked like a Gothic cathedral made of crystal. There were other buildings all made of crystal. I realized I was looking at a crystal city. These buildings represented the various architectures known on earth: Greek, Egyptian and Babylonian were the most dominant types in addition to the Gothic structures we attribute to the Middle Ages on earth. One particular building looked like the sketches of Herod's Temple I'd seen in my historical research books. Nearly every great European cathedral from the Middle Ages was represented. There were onion domes such as exist in Russia and in the Middle East, Chinese pagoda rooflines were represented, as well as the spires seen in Indonesia, Thailand and Tibet. I remember thinking of the line in the Lord's Prayer that says, ". . . on earth as it is in heaven."

I realized that the city was not crystal but light. It glittered with a life, an impossibly strong energy of its own. It was as if the buildings were living beings. I sensed the presence of other souls and angels in those buildings but did not see anyone. I did not hear music but did hear the rushing water sound of the river behind me. I realize now it was not water or the "humming" my father described in his near-death experience, rather it was energy crackling. Still, it sounded powerful like a mountain river. Once you have heard this sound, it is most memorable. I will never forget that sound.

I was in heaven, and I could not imagine ever wanting any other kind of life for myself. Instantly, a new thought entered my mind/soul/heart/being.

"You are sending me back," I stated.

"Yes."

"I like it here."

"You cannot stay. Remember to tell them, 'All is One.'"

In the moment that he said this, I felt as if I was filled again with even more knowledge. A flood of information came to me. I knew that all beings of the earth and the vast beyond and the Other Side were one of the same heart and soul. All of us are connected to each other.

"Whatsoever you do to the least of my brethren, so you do unto me." Those words of Jesus from Matthew 25:40 reverberated through my consciousness. I knew that the lowliest insect was not lowly to God. I knew that we are all equal in God's eyes. Trees, plants, animals, fish, humans and angels are all God's creations, and he loves us all. We should love and respect each other as much. Our evolution will depend on our ability to be tolerant of each other, to love one another and not to judge ourselves or others so harshly.

Humans have fallen into the pit of believing that we are cut off from God, but we never are. We are part of God, and he is within us. Our divine energy is unending. We will never die. Our bodies that hold our souls may wither and become dust, but our energy will live in the life on the Other Side. We will live forever, just not in our present body and not in our present lifetime.

One of my greatest remembrances of this experience was thinking, or rather "knowing," that there was no one religion that was any better or more right than another. My interpretation of my experience was to be tolerant of all people and to let them each find their way to God. Some Christians believe they have the "right path" to God and perhaps they do. I was not told this one way or the other. This Light Being that I perceived as Jesus and who to this day I believe was Jesus did not tell me that Christians were more right than any other religion. Actually, I suppose I expected to hear this, but I did not. At no time was there any kind of remonstration from him.

Therefore, I have no definitive answer from my experience that sheds any light on this question. Some philosophers and theologians believe that in near-death experiences, the divine in man takes on the form of the belief system of the believer. Therefore, one of the Hindu religion would see Shiva, a Buddhist would see the Buddha, and so on. Some scientists believe that there is no "experience" at all, but simply a "trigger" that is set off in the part of the brain just above the right temple that activates these visions. Perhaps that is true as well. But then, no one said heaven was a planet. And even if it was, why couldn't we go there with our brain energy/power?

The next thing I knew, I was in the recovery room in the hospital. I heard a nurse waking me up. I remember wanting to know what time it was, but I don't know why I needed to know this. In fact, I had the nurse prop me up so that I could stare at the huge clock on the wall. Perhaps it was a way of reorienting myself to earth after being in a timeless dimension. Though my eyes kept closing, I struggled to stare at the minute hand.

The next day in my room the doctor informed me that, miraculously, the tumor was benign. He had fully expected it to be malignant because it came out of nowhere and was so aggressive in its growth. There would be no need for chemotherapy, which we had believed would be the next step.

Shockingly, my recovery, which should have been six weeks, took less than two. Three weeks after the surgery my husband asked for a divorce, just as I had predicted he would. Our house went up for sale, he took back my car, and I began moving my things out before I was medically "allowed" to lift things or drive. By Christmas, which was only a few months later, I was divorced and had moved into a lovely townhouse.

On Valentine's Day my father died. (The story of my father's death and his revelations about life on the Other Side are contained in my first angel book, *Angel Watch.*)

My life as I had known it for well over a decade was over, and my new life had begun. Miraculously for me, I left my marriage without anger and hate. I needed strength to let go of my bitterness and self-pity. I accepted that God's hand was working in my life and that of my ex-husband's. God wanted divergently different futures for us, and when we surrender to God's will, the impossible becomes possible.

From my near-death experience I knew that God wanted my life to undergo this drastic alteration. Though I didn't know all the reasons for this disruption, I had faith in God that his plan for me was made in love. I trusted in God to take care of my needs and me. I knew that somehow I would not only survive, but also thrive.

Every day of my life now, I am filled with an even stronger sense of connection to everyone and everything around me. My awe of the universe and the promise of hope that it holds for all of us continues to grow.

"All is One."

On both sides of the Veil.

AUTHOR'S NOTE: *April 2005. For centuries modern man has used the guidelines of the Shroud of Turin as the blueprint of a tall, six-foot or more man with a long angular face, sharp cheekbones and jawline and long flowing hair, usually painted as red or auburn-colored. These illustrations are also in agreement with the Essene sect of the House of David to which Mary and Joseph both belonged, according to some scholars. The Essenes lived not far from Qumran where the Dead Sea Scrolls were discovered.*

According to the Encyclopaedia Britannica *(15th edition),*
". . . the Essenes established a monastic community at Qumran
in the mid-2nd century BC during the reign of Simon but no later
than the time of John Hyrcanus. After a brief reign of Herod the
Great, the community resumed its life at Qumran until the center
was destroyed (AD 68) by Roman legions under Vespasian.
Living apart, like other Essenic communities in Judaca, the 4,000
or so members of the Qumran community turned to apocalyptic
visions of the overthrow of the wicked priests of Jerusalem and
the ultimate establishment of their own community as the true
priesthood and the true Israel. They devoted their time to study of
the Scriptures, manual labor, worship and prayer. Meals were
taken in common as prophetic celebrations of the Messianic ban-
quet. The baptism they practiced symbolized repentance and
entry into the company of the 'Elect of God'."

The Shroud of Turin is supposedly the burial linen used to
bury Jesus of Nazareth after his crucifixion. The shroud is
fourteen feet long and three and a half feet wide. In 1988 a
small fragment of the Shroud of Turin was examined by the
first carbon dating of that linen. The report stated that the
shroud dated to circa AD 1200 or 1300.

In February 2005 I discovered the following information
about the Shroud of Turin. The information below was
accessed on the Internet by searching for "Shroud of Turin."
All of this information is available online. What I am includ-
ing here is just a sample.

- *January 20, 2005: "The scholarly, peer-reviewed scien-*
  tific journal Thermochimica Acta *(volume 425, pages*
  189–94, by Raymond N. Rogers, Los Alamos National

*Library University of California) makes it perfectly clear:
the carbon 14 dating sample cut from the shroud in 1988
was NOT valid. The shroud is much older than the carbon
14 dating suggests." Rogers analyzed the amount of
vanillin, a chemical compound that is present in linen
from the flax fibers used to weave it. Vanillin slowly dis-
appears from the giver over time at a* calculated rate.
*Judging by those calculations, a medieval cloth should
have 37% of its vanillin left by 1988, the year the threads
were taken from the cloth. But there was virtually none left
. . . indicating [that it is] possibly some 3,000 years old."*
- *ABC News Report: "Rome. 1/21/2005. A chemist who
worked on the testing of the Shroud of Turin says new
analysis of fiber content of the cloth that some say was the
burial linen of Jesus, could be 3,000 years old."*

*There are several articles online of the various studies
being conducted on the shroud that are difficult for the layper-
son to understand. However, one such article states that new
studies reveal not only that the Shroud of Turin was the burial
cloth of Jesus, but that other chemical breakdowns, analysis of
the blood, and so on show that this cloth was used only for a
short time. These further studies are being conducted to prove
that the Resurrection was and is a historical fact. In other
words, the cloth did not stay wrapped around this body for
long, or the body was moved and wrapped in other linen.*

*I have included all of this information and encourage you
to read more on these scientific studies only because in my
near-death experience, I witnessed a being that I believed to
be Jesus. My "experience" or "vision" appears to be*

substantiated in April 2005 by the ongoing studies of the Shroud of Turin and by many scholars who are always in search of the historical Jesus.

Namaste

AUTHOR'S NOTE: *In 2005, my friend Judy Fry, of Scottsdale, Arizona, told this story to me. Judy is a lawyer and retired judge.*

n 1987, my father died around St. Valentine's Day. I had gotten the phone call from the hospital that he'd suffered a massive stroke.

The doctor met me at the emergency room where they were working on my dad. The doctor explained that the stroke was very bad, however, they could give my father the medications that he was currently taking for blood pressure, blood thinning, and so on, and that would keep him alive. If he survived, he would be in a vegetative state at best. If they deprived him of all medications, then he would surely die from the swelling in his brain.

I am a former judge. Knowing the law and making decisions was what my professional life had been about. This moment was horrific for me. If I declined the medications, Dad would die in a few hours, surely in a day or two. If I chose the medications, his body would live, but I believed my dad would cease to exist.

The doctor pressed me for a decision right then. I thought I heard my own skull crack in two under the weight of this momentous decision. I told the doctor I needed some time to think. I went out into the waiting room of the hospital and sank to the floor. I cried and prayed to God to send me a sign of what the right decision might be. At that very moment a man approached me and said, "Do you recognize me?"

"No, I don't," I replied.

"You put me in jail for a DUI."

What would he say next? I wondered.

"You changed my life with your words the day of my sentencing. I want you to meet my family. Your decision to put me in jail changed my life for the better."

I couldn't believe it! I was at the lowest point in my life. I had put this man in jail, and yet he embraced me. He was comforting me. I realized right then and there that I had the knowledge and intuition needed to make good decisions even if they appeared to be "bad" ones. I realized at that moment that this man's comforting me was a sign from God, that I should do what I did as a judge and rely upon fairness, wisdom and my intuition to make a decision when it came to my dad.

I couldn't help but wonder if this man hadn't been sent to me by the angels years ago so that he could return to me on the day of my father's death and give me words of confirmation I so needed to hear.

I went back in to speak to the doctor.

My mouth was so dry when I spoke, I felt as if my tongue could barely get the words out. "No medications," I said.

The doctor nodded solemnly, then raced through the doors to attend to my father.

I stayed with my father for two days. Finally, I was so exhausted I had to go home and rest. As soon as I got home the doctor called and said that my father had passed.

I laid down on my bed. I was crying and tumbled into an abyss of heartbreak and grief. I sobbed for a long time, *but I did not fall asleep. It is important to understand that I was fully conscious and awake when the following happened.*

I opened my eyes after crying so hard and saw every hue and tone of the color purple that exists on earth. I saw people moving about. They looked like photographic negatives but the light and the dark were reversed. The room was filled with hundreds of people moving all around me. My father emerged from the crowd.

My father spoke to me. "I want to show you what happened to me."

Suddenly, I was "flying" with my father to the Black Angus restaurant where he had had the stroke.

I was very high above the action, sitting in the rafters of the building. My father's spirit was sitting next to me, and yet I saw him below me, choking at first, then grimacing in extreme discomfort and pain as the stroke progressed. I saw my father's friend try to help him. I saw the paramedics arrive and begin to work on him. I watched as they did all they could and then put him on a gurney. I heard every encouraging word they spoke to get through to him. I watched as they put him in the ambulance.

Suddenly I was aware that I was back in my room. I then saw both my parents in the crowd. My mother was on my left side and my father was on my right side. They said, "We want to show you what is on the Other Side, so you will recognize it when your time comes."

I left my body and "flew" with them into a tunnel with a

light at the end, kind of like the light from the headlights of a car. I went into the tunnel and walked toward the most brilliant light I have ever seen or experienced.

At the end of the tunnel was a godlike or Jesuslike figure with outstretched arms. He was radiating light, love and peace. His embrace engulfed me.

I cannot fully, accurately or completely explain what it was like to be "in this light." First of all, I was completely, physically inside this light. I had no body on the Other Side. I felt warm and absolutely unconditionally *loved*. It was overwhelming and wondrous. I was "one" with this being.

My parents took me to several areas where I saw people writing, painting, sewing, working and doing all kinds of things they loved. The houses looked like large dollhouses, because there were only three walls and the front wall was missing. There were no ceilings on any buildings.

I also remember that the clouds were the whitest of white and extremely bright, as I looked upward and saw sunshine and open sky while in the buildings.

At this point I was aware that I was being shown where my father would be and where my mother already was. He would be here with these loving, friendly people doing something he loved very much. His new life on the Other Side would be sheer bliss.

After I visited this place with no ceilings and saw many happy souls working at their artistic, talented "soul level," my parents took me back to the tunnel. I was keenly observant at this point, because I wanted to investigate this "tunnel." Now the tunnel was dark, and it looked like a round, corrugated steel sewer tunnel.

Suddenly, my mother, who had passed away when I was thirty-two, was miraculously again on my left side and my father was on my right side. They told me, telepathically, that they would be there to greet me when I came through the tunnel (upon my death).

I went into the tunnel as a spirit, but as I advanced toward earth, a substance with the consistency of Play-Doh enveloped me and created my human form.

I glanced back at my parents for one last time. Both of my parents were standing with their hands folded in a prayerlike position, and they bowed toward me from the waist and said, "Na-ma-stay, Judith Ann."

I had no idea what this word meant. Later, I went through all my foreign language dictionaries: French, Spanish, Italian, Portuguese, trying to find it.

During the ceremony for my father's passing, the minister's wife talked with me about a near-death experience she had. She told me that she had seen the same purple lights and the same photographic negative reversal of light and dark impressions that I had experienced.

She told me that Namaste is a Sanskrit word, which is the oldest recorded language on earth. It means: *I honor that place in you in which love, light and peace reside; and when you are in that place in you and I am in that place in me, there is only one of us.* On hearing that definition, I immediately remembered the feeling of oneness I felt when I "arrived" on the Other Side, and was embraced by this godlike being. I realized that I would not be separated from that being or my parents, as long as I lived my life on earth from a place of love, light and peace.

A few weeks later, I "returned" with my cousin to the Black Angus restaurant where my father fell ill. I had told her all about my vision, and I wanted her there while I verified it with the people who witnessed it firsthand.

The manager verified every aspect of my vision as accurate. Later, at the hospital, I spoke with the paramedics. Every iota of my vision was exactly as it had happened. By verifying those aspects of my vision that were worldly, I felt confident that those aspects that were otherworldly were accurate as well. I knew I had made the right decision for my father and that he was in a better place.

When one thinks of life as this great, perfect and divine dance of humans and spirits, and if we trust that everything happens according to God's divine order, then our tragedies can be seen as blessings and our mistakes (such as that man's DUI) can be seen as opportunities. There is peace in acceptance, there is love in letting go, and there is light and darkness.

This experience taught me that we are truly spiritual beings having a human experience. The next time I see that light, I will run into it because I know the wondrous feeling I will have when I am reunited with the Creator and my creators, my parents.

Feathers
for
Thought

An angel's wing is made up of bone, flesh and feathers. In addition to my own account of seeing an actual angel during my NDE on the operating table, to the many stories I've gleaned from interviews with others who have seen a winged angel, I have my own validation that angels do exist.

I touched an angel's wing, and I distinctly remember what that wing felt like. I can always tell if someone is telling me the truth by the way they describe that wing and those feathers. If it substantiates my own experience then I believe what they are telling is fact, not fiction.

As I write this book, there are many stories that are only snippets. They aren't long enough to devote an entire chapter to, but they are just as important to the understanding of the kinship between humans and angels as knowing there truly *are* feathers on an angel's wing.

These then, are my feathers for you to ponder.

Sam and George

My nephew Sam was about two and a half years old when he went through a bout of sleeplessness. Every morning he would come downstairs still in his sleeper pajamas complaining about his lack of sleep.

One morning in particular, my sister, Nancy, was making waffles for breakfast, when Sammy came to the kitchen and crawled up onto the white painted wood chair, rubbing his eyes and yawning.

"What's the matter, Sam? Can't sleep?" She ruffled his thick hair and kissed his cheek.

"No, Mommie."

"Are you sick?" She laid her hand on his forehead. "No fever."

"I don't feel sick."

"Maybe it's your throat."

"Mommie, I'm fine. I just can't sleep." He stretched and yawned.

Nancy placed his waffle in front of him and sat in the chair beside him. "Maybe it's too much television before bed."

"Maybe it's George."

"George? Who is George? A new cartoon on TV?" Nancy asked.

"No, Mommie. He's my friend. George. From Canada."

"You met a new friend at Step Ahead?"

"No, Mommie," Sammy stuffed his mouth with waffle.

"Does he telephone you at night that I don't know about?" Nancy was truly puzzled.

"Oh, Mommie. You know Daddy doesn't let us talk on the phone at night. He said it was a rule because his patients need him."

"That's right. But how does George bother you?"

"He comes to visit, and he just talks all the time," Sammy complained.

"Comes to visit?" Nancy was alarmed. "How?"

By this time Sammy was getting exasperated with his mother's lack of understanding. "I don't know how. He's just in my room."

Nancy felt goose bumps. "George from Canada. Hmmm. There's no one who has moved to the neighborhood recently."

"Mommie! You know . . . George. George in the silver pajamas."

Silver pajamas!!!

"Sammy, tonight you sleep in our room. Maybe George will leave you alone from now on."

"Okay, Mommie!" Sammy went back to his waffle.

That night, Sammy slept with Nancy and Dave. There were no more stories of George from Canada in the silver pajamas.

Mouths of Babes

Christmas 1994.

was in Marshall Field's downtown store on State Street in Chicago with my sister, Nancy, her daughter, Elaine, and son, Sam, who was six years old at the time.

Nancy and Elaine were looking at hair ribbons and headbands, so I took Sam to the other side of the store to look at sunglasses.

Sammy tried on several pairs, and out of the blue, he said, "Aunt Cathy, do you remember when we lived in the big city, and we used to watch boxing on television?"

I said, "Gee, no, Sam. What big city? You mean New York?"

"Yes, New York."

I could not figure out what he was talking about. I'd never been to New York with Sam.

"Don't you remember, Aunt Cathy? We ate our dinner in the silver dishes."

This really threw me. "We were rich?"

"Not that kind of silver dish. You know, with the spaces for the chicken, corn and mashed potatoes."

Then it hit me. TV dinners!

Now, my sister, Nancy, has never served a TV dinner in her life. This woman bakes her own French bread and makes waffles from scratch on a nearly daily basis for her children. Nancy is the ultimate gourmet cook. Frankly, I'm not sure Nancy knows they still make TV dinners.

I realized then that Sam was talking about his past life, or another life, and somehow he remembered I was there. I have no memory of this, but Sam was adamant about the situation and the specifics.

I followed up this story with some research of my own. In the late 1930s and early 1940s New York City was experimenting with "closed circuit television" and one of the programs available to New York City residents only were boxing matches on Wednesday nights. In addition, frozen foods were common in the late 1920s when Bird's Eye Corporation invested in the process. Dinners packaged by companies like Swanson were in distribution before World War II.

Make of it what you will, dear reader.

The Long Car

My granddaughter, Caylin, comes about once a month to spend the night with me or sometimes, if we are very lucky, a couple nights. She loves sleeping in my huge, king-sized bed with me, cuddled with lots of pillows and the stuffed animals I keep for her at my house. We watch *Cinderella* together, play with the dollhouse I made for her and read lots of books. It's our time for me to pamper her, talk together and learn about each other. I treasure these moments and hours like none other in my life.

This particular night, Caylin woke up about three in the morning to go to the bathroom. Our talking and rumbling around in the bedroom and bathroom woke up my dogs, Bebe and Junior, who came running up the stairs to see the action. I quieted them down, and then Caylin and I returned to bed. After playing with the dogs and getting a drink of water, we were both truly awake at this time.

Caylin was lying on her back holding her soft, stuffed puppy above her in the air, singing to it with the lights on when she said, "Cathy, do you remember when we lived before?"

As she said this, I noticed that her voice was different

somehow and that she did not address me as Grandma Cathy as she ordinarily did. Chills raced down my spine when my unsettled mind locked onto the key to my piqued interest.

"Before?" I asked the word very carefully, wondering if I had heard her correctly.

"Yes. When we lived in the big city and rode in the long car?" At this she turned and looked at me with probing eyes. Eyes not of a child.

I was stunned at this point. Twice in my life this had happened. A child close to me in their early years, before the age of seven, and Sammy in particular, had asked me about this other lifetime "in the big city."

"No, I don't," I replied.

"Well, I do. It was fun. I liked that car."

I did not pursue this line of questioning. I guess I was so stunned this came from my granddaughter, yet I don't know why.

Then she rolled onto her side and touched my face in the way you do with someone you remember very well, or someone you are saying good-bye to forever. It was a deep knowing look of recognition that I'd witnessed from an adult, but not a three-year-old child.

"I wuv you," she said. Then she kissed me, and again I was struck by the idea that this was the kind of kiss you give someone when they are dying or leaving your life. It was incredibly sad, and I felt my heart ripping because I could not remember who she was in that life we had shared together.

"I love you, too," I said.

"Let's say our prayers again, okay?" she asked.

And we did.

Today, I am certain that Caylin has no remembrance of that night or the memory she had of our past life together. She was only three, and her mind was obviously open to her past life.

This incident took place nearly four years ago, and despite my own near-death experiences and interaction with angels and departed loved ones, this experience with Caylin is still one of the most haunting incidents in my life.

Again, I believe that I have proof that we never leave our love behind. We never truly abandon the ones who have loved us and that we love.

The lesson here is that when given a day in our lives to breathe, make very certain you have filled your every moment with love. To give love and receive love is why we were given life by our Creator.

Use your moments wisely and lovingly.

Dominic and the Light

AUTHOR'S NOTE: *This is another story from Jim Keating.*

One day my wife, Clare, was teaching her junior high school class when she was called to the administration office. Once there, she received a sad phone call from her mother in Oklahoma. Clare's parents had been vacationing, pulling a house trailer through the Southwest on their way to Mexico. During a rest stop, their dog had escaped and started to chase after some horses. Clare's father took chase after the dog, which he retrieved. When he came back to the car, he said, "I don't feel very well." A few minutes later, Clare's father died of a very sudden heart attack.

Our children were all in elementary school classes that day, and rather than contact them, Clare decided that we should wait until they all returned home from school to break the news.

Dominic, our second eldest child, was the first to arrive at home.

"Something strange happened today at school," he said. "I was sitting at my desk in the back of the room when I saw a small ball of light in the front of the room. It seemed to be looking around, but no one else saw this light. I told the light with my mind that it could come to be by me. It came over to my side and then came into my chest. My arms seemed to glow. It stayed with me for less than a minute. It was scary. It seemed comfortable. Then, it went quickly out the window."

When Clare asked Dominic what time this event happened, she realized that it was shortly after her father had passed over.

Upon reflection, both Clare and I felt that her father was coming to check on his grandkids and Dominic had the sensitivity to see his light, though he did not realize it was his grandfather.

Even to this day, there is no question that our son saw his grandfather's soul that day.

Faeries and Angels

AUTHOR'S NOTE: *This story was recently sent to me by Jim Keating. These stories about angelic visitations to children, I believe, are some of the most fascinating.*

*O*ne weekend morning, Clare was in the kitchen making pancakes, and our oldest son, Jim, about four at the time, came out of his bedroom and said his fairy godmother had just appeared to him. Clare was fascinated and asked him to explain. He said he was lying in bed, and suddenly there was a bright yellow light with specks in it next to his bed. The light was cold. This got Clare's attention.

Then he said she appeared in the light.

Clare asked if her hair was long.

"No," he said "It was short like yours [about to the ears]."

Upon further questioning, his description did not fit the typical picture of a Disney fairy godmother. He said her dress came only to midthigh, the sleeves on her top came just over the shoulder and there was a large belt. Clare thought it sounded like a tunic. He continued that she had stockings that were evidently something similar to today's leotards.

Clare asked if he was sure it was a female. "Did she have breasts?"

He said, "I guess so, but I couldn't see them. She was looking at me, and I didn't want her to know I was awake. I was lying on my side and kept my top eye closed and looked at her with my bottom eye. Then she disappeared, and the light was gone too."

When I awoke, Jim repeated his story to me. His sincerity and matter-of-fact manner convinced Clare and me that he was telling the truth that something special had happened. I got out a tape recorder and asked him to repeat the experience one more time.

Reluctantly, he did so, but then did not want to talk about it anymore. Clare and I both believe he was not seeking attention and that this incident was real.

Postscript

ear Reader,

I hope you enjoyed this second book in our series of angel stories. It is my desire to continue bringing these kinds of hopeful and inspiring messages to you. As you know from reading this book, most of the stories come from either my own family or from family friends. In the future, I would like to change that perspective.

If you have a story of angelic intervention or an "inexplicable" miracle that has happened in your life, and you would like to share it with me, I would truly be interested in printing your story in my third book in this series.

You can e-mail your complete story to me at: *cathlanigan@yahoo.com* or mail it to: Catherine Lanigan, 2554 Lincoln Boulevard, P.O. Box 295, Marina del Rey, CA 90291.

If you believe as I do that there are angels all around us, then please help me get the message to those who need guidance, hope and faith in their lives but don't know where or how to find it. I am most interested in your input and your contributions to future books in this series.

Thank you for all your support over the years and for reminding your friends to keep their own "angel watch."

Blessings,
Catherine

Bibliography

Alper, Matthew. *The God Part of the Brain.* (New York: Rogue Press, 2000).

Bell, Art, and Brad Steiger. *The Source.* (New Orleans: Paper Chase Press, 1999).

Braden, Gregg. *The Isaiah Effect.* (New York: Harmony Books, 2000).

Brinkley, Dannion. *Saved by the Light.* (New York: Harper, 1995).

Bro, Harmon Hartzell. *A Seer Out of Season: The Life of Edgar Cayce.* (New York: Signet, 1990).

Cayce, Hugh Lynn. *The Edgar Cayce Collection: Edgar Cayce on Dreams; Edgar Cayce on Healing; Edgar Cayce on Diet and Health; Edgar Cayce on ESP.* (New York: Bonanza Books, 1986).

Cerminara, Gina. *Many Mansions: The Edgar Cayce Story.* (New York: Signet, 1950).

Eusebius. *The History of the Church.* (New York: Dorset Press, 1965).

Faraday, Dr. Anne. *Dream Power: Learn to Use the Vital Self-Knowledge that Lies Stored in your Dreams.* (New York: Berkley, 1972).

Fiore, Edith. *You Have Been Here Before: A Psychologist Looks at Past Lives.* (New York: Ballantine, 1978).

Furst, Jeffery, ed. *Edgar Cayce's Story of Jesus.* (New York: Berkley, 1976).

Goodwin, Malcolm. *Angels: An Endangered Species.* (New York: Simon and Schuster, 1990).

Goldberg, Dr. Bruce. *Past Lives, Future Lives.* (New York: Ballantine, 1982).

Graham, Billy. *Angels.* (Dallas: Word Publishing, 1975).

Hancock, Graham. *Fingerprints of the Gods.* (New York: Three Rivers Press, 1995).

Harris, Errol E. *The Reality of Time.* (Albany, NY: State University of New York Press, 1988).

Hegel, G. W. F. *Phenomenology of Mind.* Trans. J. Baillie. (London: G. Allen and Unwin, reprint, 1966).

Heidegger, Martin. *Holzwege. (*Frankfort, Germany: Frankfort-am-Main, 1952).

Hillman, James. *The Soul's Code. (*New York: Warner Books, 1997).

Holmes, Ernest. *The Science of Mind.* (New York: Dodd, Mead and Company, 1938).

Houston, Jean. *The Search for the Beloved.* (New York: St. Martin's Press, 1987).

Janes, Julian. *The Origin of Consciousness in the Breakdown of the Bicameral Mind.* (Boston: Houghton Mifflin, 1976).

Kenyon, Tom. *Brain States.* (Naples, FL: United States Publishing, 1994).

Krapf, Phillip H. *The Contact Has Begun.* (Carlsbad, CA: Hay House, 1998).

Mandino, Og. *The Greatest Salesman in the World; The Greatest Secret in the World; The Greatest Miracle in the World.* (New York: Bonanza Books, 1981).

McDannell, Colleen, and Bernhard Lang. *Heaven: A History.* (New York: Vintage, 1990).

Moody, Raymond A., Jr. *Coming Back: A Psychiatrist Explores Past-Life Journeys.* (New York: Bantam, 1991).

———. *Life After Life.* (New York: Bantam. Mockingbird Books, 1976).

Morse, Melvin. *Closer to the Light: Learning from Children's Near Death Experiences.* (New York: Random House, 1990).

Morse, Melvin, and Paul Perry. *Where God Lives.* (New York: HarperCollins, 2000).

Peale, Norman Vincent. *Positive Imaging.* (New York: Fawcett, 1982).

Peck, M. Scott. *In Heaven as on Earth.* (New York, Hyperion, 1996).

———. *People of the Lie: The Hope for Healing Human Evil.* (New York: Hyperion, 1989).

Ponder, Catherine. *The Dynamic Laws of Prosperity.* (Marina Del Ray, CA: DeVorss and Company, 1962).

Prophet, Elizabeth Clare. *Violet Flame to Heal Body, Mind and Soul.* (Corwin Springs, MT: Summit University Press, 1997).

Rawlings, Dr. Maurice. *Beyond Death's Door.* (New York: Bantam Books, 1978).

Reed, Henry. *Edgar Cayce on Mysteries of the Mind.* (New York: Warner, 1989).

Ring, Kenneth. *Heading Toward Omega.* (New York: Morrow, 1990).

———. *The Omega Project.* (New York: Morrow, 1992).

Schlotterbeck, Karl. *Living Your Past Lives: The Psychology of Past Life Regression.* (New York: Ballantine, 1989).

Sheldrake, Rupert. *A New Science of Life: The Hypothesis for Formative Causation.* (Boston: Houghton Mifflin, 1981).

Steiger, Brad. *Guardian Angels and Spirit Guides.* (New York: Signet, 1995).

Steiger, Brad and Francie. *The Star People.* (New York: Berkley, 1981).

Strean, Dr. Herbert, and Lucy Freeman. *The Severed Soul.* (New York: St. Martin's Press, 1990).

Teilhard de Chardin, P. *The Phenomenon of Man.* Translated by B. Wall. Introduced by Julian Huxley. (New York: Harper and Row, 1959).

Twitchell, Paul. *Eckankar: The Key to Secret Worlds.* (Crystal, MN: Illuminated Way Publishing, 1969).

———. *The Eck-Vidya.* (Minneapolis: Eckankar, 1972).

Van Praagh, James. *Reaching to Heaven.* (New York: Dutton, 1999).

———. *Talking to Heaven.* (New York: Signet, 1999).

Walsch, Neale Donald. *Conversations with God: Book 1.* (Charlottesville, VA: Hampton Roads Publishing, 1998).

Walsh, Michael. *Butler's Lives of the Saints.* (San Francisco: Harper and Row, 1956; reprint, 1987).

———. *Conversations with God: Book 2.* (Charlottesville, VA: Hampton Roads Publishing, 1997).

———. *Conversations with God: Book 3.* (Charlottesville, VA: Hampton Roads Publishing, 1998).

Weiss, Brian L. *Many Lives, Many Masters.* (New York: Fireside, 1988).

Wills-Brandon, Carla. *One Last Hug Before I Go: The Mystery and Meaning of Deathbed Visions.* (Deerfield Beach, FL: Health Communications, 2001).

Wilson, Colin. *C. G. Jung: Lord of the Underworld.* (Wellingsborough, England: Thorsons Publishing Group, 1984).

Zukav, Gary. *The Seat of the Soul.* (New York: Fireside, 1990).

Code #8199 • $11.95

In this thought-provoking collection of
true-life miracles, Catherine Lanigan reveals how we
all can travel through life on active angel watch.